Building Foundat... Marriage: A Pre-Ma......... Counseling Study

The Bible Teacher's Guide

Gregory Brown

B▮G
Publishing

Endorsements

"Expositional, theological, and candidly practical! I highly recommend *The Bible Teacher's Guide* for anyone seeking to better understand or teach God's Word."

—Dr. Young–Gil Kim, Founding President of Handong Global University

"Greg Brown's *The Bible Teacher's Guide* is a wonderful resource for the whole body of Christ. These guides are clear, easy to read, and very user friendly. Whether you are preparing a Bible study, a sermon, or simply wanting to dive deeper into a personal study of God's Word, these will be very helpful tools."

—Eddie Byun, Professor of Practical Theology at Torch Trinity Graduate University; Author of *Justice Awakening*

"The best Bible teaching guides come from those who are already skillful teachers. I have found that teaching younger people is particularly helpful preparation for a wider Bible teaching ministry because one has to labor to keep the attention of the students and apply truth relevantly and vibrantly to their lives. Greg Brown has all these qualifications. A week of concentrated teaching to students from his ministry gave me evidence of the very effective work he is doing among university students in Korea. I am happy that Greg is making his insights into God's truth available to a wider audience through these books. They bear the hallmarks of good Bible teaching: the result of rigorous Bible study and thoroughgoing application to the lives of people."

—Ajith Fernando, Teaching Director, Youth for Christ; Author of *A Call to Joy and Pain*

"Gregory Brown has created a user–friendly resource for Bible study. *The Bible Teacher's Guide* is thorough but concise, with thought–provoking discussion questions in each section. This is a great tool for teaching God's Word."

—Dr. Steve Pettey, Dean of Louisiana Baptist Theological Seminary

"The format (pertinent questions related directly to the text) draws the reader into the content of the passage while at the same time modeling sound interpretive method. Knowing the right questions to ask and how to go about answering them is fundamental to learning in any subject matter. Greg demonstrates this convincingly."

—Dr. William Moulder, Professor of Biblical Studies at Trinity International University

"Greg Brown's *The Bible Teacher's Guide* is thorough, scholarly enough to explain the text, clear, and practical. He treats difficult verses fairly and with helpful explanations (unlike many commentaries that skip the explanation right where you want it!). This study could be used by pastors as an aid for sermon preparation, by small group leaders, or by any believer who wants to understand and apply God's Word personally. I can't imagine any student of Scripture not benefiting by this work."

—Steven J. Cole, Pastor, Flagstaff Christian Fellowship, Author of the *Riches from the Word* series

"Greg has a scholar's mind, a pastor's heart, and an athlete's body. *The Bible Teacher's Guide* series is scholarly enough for pastors and is pastorally helpful for anyone who wants to study or teach the Bible. The content of the series is rich. My prayer is that God will use it to help the body of Christ grow strong."

—Dr. Min Chung, Senior Pastor of Covenant Fellowship Church (Urbana, Illinois)

"For several years, it has been my joy to hear the teachings of Greg Brown. Pastor Greg is passionate about the Word of God, rigorous and thorough in his approach to the study of it, and consistent in his life that exemplifies what he preaches. I am pleased to recommend *The Bible Teacher's Guide* to anyone who hungers for the living Word."

—Dr. JunMo Cho, Worship Leader and Recording Artist; Professor of Linguistics at Handong Global University

4

Contents

Preface

And the things you have heard me say in the presence of many witnesses entrust to reliable men who will also be qualified to teach others.
2 Timothy 2:2

Paul's words to Timothy still apply to us today. There is a need to raise up teachers who will correctly handle the Word and fearlessly teach the Word. It is with this hope in mind that the Bible Teachers Guide (BTG) series has been created. The BTG series includes both expositional book studies and topical studies. This guide will be useful for individual study, small groups, and for teachers preparing to share God's Word.

Building Foundations for a Godly Marriage can be used as an eight-week small group study on marriage, a pre-marital or marital counseling curriculum, or simply to help one have a deeper understanding of marriage. It is good for pre-married couples, married couples, and singles studying the topic in a small group. Every week the members of the small group will read a chapter, complete the homework questions, and be prepared to share in the small group gathering. Because each member will prepare for the small group, this will enrich the discussion and the learning. For further tips on small group format see Appendixes 4 and 5.

I pray that the Lord may richly bless your study and use it to build his kingdom.

Introduction

Welcome! The fact you chose to do this study means you care about having a godly marriage, one that pleases the Lord. The focus of this study will be biblical premarital counseling, but the principles taught will be great for married couples as well. Unlike many premarital courses, we will not be focusing on psychology but on the Bible. We will do this because we believe in the sufficiency of Scripture. Second Timothy 3:16-17 says: "All Scripture is God-breathed and is useful for teaching, rebuking, correcting and training in righteousness, so that the man of God may be thoroughly equipped for every good work."

The "good work" Scripture will prepare you for through this study is marriage. God made marriage (Gen 1:27). He ordained it; it is meant to reflect him (cf. 1 Cor 11:3, Eph 5:22-27), and he gives instructions in his Word on how it should be developed and maintained.

In this study, we will consider eight foundations for a godly marriage: God's plan, gender roles, commitment, communication, conflict resolution, training children, finances, and intimacy. Like the foundation of any building, if there are cracks structurally, the house will have problems and may not last. As mentioned, each of these foundations will be built or restored using the Word of God. In speaking about the Christian's life, Christ said the house built on the rock of his Word will stand (Matt 7:24-25). Certainly, this is true of marriages as well.

Overview:

This will be a demanding study. For counseling purposes, this is best completed along with your mate under a mentor or a mentor couple. However, this study will also be a blessing to those studying individually or in a small group. The expectations for each session are as follows:

1. Read the lesson and complete the homework individually.
2. Discuss the answers to the homework with your mate (and/or small group).
3. Discuss the answers with a mentor or a mentor couple to gain their insight and counsel if at all possible.

This study is eight sessions. You should aim to complete at least one session a week. For further information, please look through the appendices. May God greatly enrich your study!

Foundation One: God's Plan for Marriage

> Then God said, "Let us make man in our image, in our likeness, and let them rule over the fish of the sea and the birds of the air, over the livestock, over all the earth, and over all the creatures that move along the ground." So God created man in his own image, in the image of God he created him; male and female he created them. God blessed them and said to them, "Be fruitful and increase in number; fill the earth and subdue it. Rule over the fish of the sea and the birds of the air and over every living creature that moves on the ground... The LORD God said, 'It is not good for the man to be alone. I will make a helper suitable for him.'...For this reason a man will leave his father and mother and be united to his wife, and they will become one flesh.
> Genesis 1:26-28, 2:18, 24

In this session, we will consider God's plan for marriage as primarily seen in the Genesis narrative. Most married couples miss God's best simply because they do not know what God desires for marriage. If you don't know the purpose of something, it is destined for misuse. Therefore, over 50% of marriages end in divorce, and a large number of those who remain married continue to miss God's purpose for their union.

Today, we will help move your marriage or future marriage in the direction God desires through studying his Word. In this session, we will consider five aspects of God's plan for marriage.

God's Plan for Marriage Is to Reflect His Image

> Then God said, 'Let us make man in our image, in our likeness, and let them rule over the fish of the sea and the birds of the air, over the livestock, over all the earth, and over all the creatures that move along the ground.' *So God created man in his own image, in the image of God he created him; male and female he created them.*
> Genesis 1:26-27

The Bible teaches Adam and Eve, as husband and wife, were created in the image of God and, therefore, were meant to bear God's image—to be in his likeness. Marriage was meant to model and display God's glory to all of creation.

13

In what ways is the image of God reflected in the marriage union?

We see his image is in the *plurality* and *unity* of marriage. God said, "Let us make man in our image," and then the text says, "male and female, he created them" (v. 26, 27). When God made man, he made a plurality. He made man and woman, and later in the narrative, he said they would become "one flesh" (Gen 2:24). The Trinity is God the Father, God the Son, and God the Holy Spirit; they are one and yet still individual persons. When a couple gets married, they are meant to demonstrate this. Marriage demonstrates two individual people becoming "one" for the rest of their lives while maintaining their individuality.

With that said, there are other Trinitarian implications to the marriage union. In the Trinity, Jesus the Son submits in all things to God the Father (cf. John 5:19, 1 Cor 15:27) and the Holy Spirit submits to both (cf. John 14:26, 15:26). There is perfect submission in the Godhead. In the same way, when God made man and woman in his image, there was meant to be order in the relationship. First Corinthians 11:3 says: "Now I want you to realize that the head of every man is Christ, and the head of the woman is man, and the head of Christ is God."

Paul says in the same way that the head of Christ is God, so the head of the woman (better translated wife) is man. God made the husband and wife relationship to mirror the Godhead specifically in the area of authority. Therefore, Ephesians 5:24 calls for wives to submit to their husbands in everything.

Another Trinitarian implication is love in marriage. The wife submits to the husband and the husband loves his wife. Consider Ephesians 5:25-27:

> Husbands, love your wives, just as Christ loved the church and gave himself up for her to make her holy, cleansing her by the washing with water through the word, and to present her to himself as a radiant church, without stain or wrinkle or any other blemish, but holy and blameless.

The submission of the wife happens in a perfect loving relationship with her husband. Similarly, throughout eternity, the Godhead has always dwelled in a perfect relationship of love and authority. The Father loves the Son and the Son submits to the Father. The Father does not oppress the Son and make him submit. He loves the Son, and within this perfect love, the Son submits to God. The Holy Spirit loves and submits to both. In fact, 1 John 4:8 simply says, "God is love."

In the same way, wives are called to submit to their husbands, and husbands are called to love their wives. It is not that the wife does not love her husband or that the husband never submits to his wife (cf. Eph 5:21). It's just that the defining characteristic of the woman's service to her husband should be submission, and the defining characteristic of the husband's service to his wife should be love. This is part of the way we see the image of God in the marriage relationship.

Ephesians 5:25 gives us a picture of what the husband's love should look like. It should reflect Christ. The husband is called to love his wife as Christ loved the church. How did Christ love the church? He died for her, and he also teaches her the Word of God. The husband must love his wife sacrificially and lead his wife spiritually.

When the world looks at a Christian marriage, they should see a husband who makes daily sacrifices for his wife and actively leads the home spiritually. He leads his family to a Bible preaching church. He leads family devotions. He serves his wife and edifies her with his words. He sacrifices to please her and build her up. The wife honors him as her head and submits to him in everything (Col 3:18). This is a redemptive picture of the gospel.

Marriage should demonstrate the perfect love and submission in the Godhead. It should also reflect the perfect sacrificial love of Christ for the church and the church's submission to Christ. People should be encouraged and challenged by watching a godly marriage. They should see something of the glory and the greatness of God.

Therefore, when a marriage is not functioning correctly, it displays a marred image of God and distorts its intended message. With so many marriages ending in divorce or continuing in disarray, the glory of God has been greatly dimmed. It is no surprise that so many people doubt God's existence or are falling away from him. The light in marriages has often become darkness, which in turn pushes people away from God. In marriage, it should be our desire to reflect God and bring glory to him since that was his original plan.

God Plan's for Marriage Is to Raise Godly Children

> God blessed them and said to them, 'Be fruitful and increase in number; fill the earth and subdue it.
> Genesis 1:28

At one point, raising children was considered the pinnacle of marriage and revered by all. However, many now see children as a burden and the ultimate kill-joy for a married couple and sometimes even for society. One of the key differences between angels and mankind is the fact that God made man to procreate, to create new beings as he did. When a couple relinquishes the prospect of having children for job, hobbies, freedom, etc., they are missing out on one of the grandest and most awesome desires of God for marriage. This is further supported by what God said through the prophet Malachi:

> Has not the LORD made them one? In flesh and spirit they are his. And why one? Because he was seeking godly offspring. So guard yourself in your spirit, and do not break faith with the wife of your youth.
> Malachi 2:15

This passage clarifies God's command for people to be fruitful and multiply in Genesis 1:28. It is not just children he wants but godly children. He

15

wants children who are holy and driven to see the kingdom of God advance. One of the parents' highest purposes is to teach their children the Bible, to help them grow in character, and to help them find their spiritual gifts and calling in serving the Lord.

Now, it must be noted that obviously it is not God's will for everybody to have children. Physical issues keep some from having children. For others, God simply never called for them to marry. However, in general, it has been God's will from the beginning for man to be fruitful and multiply (Gen 1:28). Having children should be considered as a way of obeying God and building his kingdom. Therefore, we should pray about it and plan for it as we do with any ministry.

God's Plan for Marriage Is to Establish and Build His Kingdom

> God blessed them and said to them... fill the earth and subdue it. Rule over the fish of the sea and the birds of the air and over every living creature that moves on the ground.
> Genesis 1:28

After telling Adam and Eve to be fruitful and multiply, God told them to subdue and rule over the earth. They were to be co-rulers over his creation and to be stewards of it. This is expanded in the New Testament as marriage is described as a spiritual gift given to build up the body of Christ and to advance his kingdom. Consider what Paul said in 1 Corinthians 7:7:

> Sometimes I wish everyone were single like me--a simpler life in many ways! But celibacy is not for everyone any more than marriage is. God gives the gift of the single life to some, the gift of the married life to others. (The Message)

Here Paul taught that marriage is a spiritual gift, just as singleness is. And since all gifts are given to build up God's body and his kingdom (cf. 1 Cor 12:7), a godly marriage is a powerful weapon for the kingdom of God. *They build the kingdom through raising godly seed, corporate prayer, service to God's church, and evangelism of the world.*

Certainly, each couple will have unique gifts and a unique way God has called them to build his kingdom. One couple may excel in worship, another in teaching, another in hospitality, another in missions, etc. Each couple must discern the way God has uniquely called them to build his kingdom.

How is God calling you and your mate to uniquely build his kingdom?

God's Plan for Marriage Is Companionship

The LORD God said, 'It is not good for the man to be alone. I will make a helper suitable for him.'
Genesis 2:18

God has put an innate desire in mankind for intimate companionship. This is why so many single people, though they have family and friends, covet something more and often have bouts of loneliness. God made man to be married to a woman and woman to a man.

Certainly some in the world have the gift of singleness, a very special gift given to allow for a deeper devotion to God and his work (cf. 1 Cor 7:32). The gift of singleness is a gift that needs to be restored to the church, as singles have accomplished some of the greatest work for God's kingdom (i.e. Jesus and Paul). But, with that said, this gift is not for everyone. God wants most people to have a mate: someone to fellowship with, to dream with, to serve with, and to be heirs of life together with. It is a beautiful experience and a great gift.

Solomon gave several reasons that companionship is good. Ecclesiastes 4:9-12 says:

Two are better than one, because they have a good return for their work: If one falls down, his friend can help him up. But pity the man who falls and has no one to help him up! Also, if two lie down together, they will keep warm. But how can one keep warm alone? Though one may be overpowered, two can defend themselves. A cord of three strands is not quickly broken.

Though these apply to any companionship, they most definitely apply to marriage. He said that two are better than one because of the *productivity of their work*. Many couples have seen themselves more productive in finishing school, working in business, growing in the Lord, doing ministry, etc., because of the marriage union. God desires to increase one's productivity through marriage.

Solomon also said that a companion is helpful when *one falls down because a friend can help him up*. Life has many ups, downs, discouragements, trials, and even mountain-top experiences. However, many times there are more downs than ups. When a marriage is working properly, it will help navigate the trials and discouragements of life. A good spouse will speak words of encouragement and faith to her mate, enabling him to get up when he has fallen down. She will make him strong when he is weak and vice versa.

Sadly, marriages that are not functioning properly will actually wear one another down instead of building one another up. Be careful to never speak words of discouragement over your spouse. Decide to always speak gracious words over their lives to edify them, even when you don't feel like it or you feel like they don't deserve it. Ephesians 4:29 says, "Do not let any unwholesome talk come out of your mouths, but only what is helpful for building others up according to their needs, that it may benefit those who listen."

17

Do you practice speaking words of faith and encouragement over your mate to help build them up?

Marriage also has many other practical benefits such as keeping oneself warm and providing for daily needs, but one of the greatest benefits is *protection*. Solomon said two can defend themselves (Ecc 4:12). This is especially important in a Christian marriage because of the attacks of the enemy in spiritual warfare. Satan realizes the tremendous potential in every marriage, and consequently, he always attacks them. Expect warfare in marriage. Satan will do everything he can to keep a couple out of the Word of God, out of prayer, away from commitment to the church, and fighting with one another. He does this because he realizes that two people unified and on fire for the kingdom of God can do incrementally more than one.

Therefore, it is important for couples to use their spiritual weapons to protect one another. These weapons are praying over one another daily, consistent Bible reading, speaking the Word of God over one another, commitment in serving the body of Christ, and having accountability with other Christians.

Have you given thought to the increased warfare that will happen in the marriage union? Many find themselves overpowered in marriage for lack of understanding the nature of their new warfare.

God's Plan for Marriage Is for a Couple to Make a New Family Unit

> For this reason a man will leave his father and mother and be united to his wife, and they will become one flesh.
> Genesis 2:24

After God made a woman for Adam, he said that a man will leave his father and mother and be united to his wife. This means that in marriage, a couple is starting a new family unit.

This does not mean that they are no longer their parents' children, but it does mean that the priorities of a man and woman have changed. Their priority must now be their marriage. This is very important because one of the top reasons for divorce is in-laws. The wife battles between submitting to her parents' expectations and that of her husband, and it's the same for the husband. Every time the couple fights, the husband's mom or the wife's father has something to say.

Married couples must be very careful of this. They are always called to honor their parents and even care for them in old age (1 Tim 5:4, 8), but they must honor their spouse first.

The fact that a man is called to leave his father's house also implies that he must be able to support himself and his new wife financially. It implies independence. Young couples who are still dependent upon their parents

18

financially often invite unnecessary tension in their marriage. The parents' financial support typically comes with a certain amount of control or expectations that can be detrimental to their marriage.

Couples who are ready to get married should consider whether they are financially prepared to get married. They should consider if they are ready to leave their families and cleave to their mate and also if they are ready to make their mate their primary focus after God.

Conclusion

In conclusion, it important to remember the reasons God created marriage, because if we forget them, the marriage relationship is destined for abuse. Instead of building God's kingdom, raising godly children, or providing companionship, couples neglect these pursuits for other things which ultimately cripple their marriage. Let us always remember God's plans for the marriage union so that we can honor them and fulfill God's purposes.

1. God's plan for marriage is to reflect his image.
2. God's plan for marriage is to raise godly children.
3. God's plan for marriage is to establish and build his kingdom.
4. God's plan for marriage is companionship.
5. God's plan for marriage is for married couples to make a new family unit.

God's Plan for Marriage Homework

Answer the questions, then discuss together.

1. What was new or stood out to you in this session? In what ways were you challenged or encouraged? Were there any points/thoughts that you did not agree with?

2. Why do you want to marry this person? Give five reasons other than love.

3. If marriage is a spiritual gift meant to advance the kingdom of God, evaluate yourself and your spiritual gifts. How has God uniquely gifted you to build up his church (teaching, encouraging, serving, helping, mercy, etc.)? If you are not sure, ask your mate or friends what they would consider your spiritual gifts to be.

4. What are your mate's spiritual gifts? How do you see God using your mate to build the kingdom of God, serve the church, etc.? How can you help him/her in that pursuit?

5. Solomon discussed some of the benefits of companionship that we find in marriage such as: being productive in work, helping when the other stumbles, and protecting one another. What are your common pitfalls or circumstances where you find yourself prone to discouragement or sin? What are the triggers to those pitfalls (problems with career, family, depression, worry, spiritual life, etc.)? How do you navigate these trials and what role can your spouse play to help you out?

6. The weapons we use in spiritual warfare and the trials of life are primarily spiritual. Discuss your spiritual disciplines (prayer, reading the Word, accountability, fasting, church attendance, service, etc.) and how you implement them daily/weekly. How do you think your mate is in his/her spiritual disciplines and how can you encourage one another in them so you can more effectively overpower the enemy?

7. God's desire for most marriages is to be fruitful and multiply, producing godly children. How many children do you want? How many does your

mate want? Have you discussed family planning? Will you use contraception? If so, what types? It is important to research this before the wedding as some methods are abortive and therefore immoral.

8. What type of relationship do you have with your parents? Do you foresee your family having any problems with your marriage (i.e. not accepting your spouse, cultural problems, distance, etc.)?

9. What type of relationship do you have with your mate's parents? In what ways do you think you could better minister to or get to know your mate's parents in order to honor them (cf. Eph 6:2)?

10. Do you foresee any problems in your marriage with putting the union first over one's parents? Explain.

11. Do your parents or your mate's parents have any serious sicknesses? God's call on couples is to care for their parents in old age (1 Tim 5:4, 8). Have you and your mate discussed the possibility of caring for parents in old age? How would you handle this? Share any thoughts or concerns.

12. After completing this session, in what ways do you feel God is calling you to pray for your future marriage? Spend some time praying.

Foundation Two: Gender Roles in Marriage

In this session, we will discuss God's roles for the husband and wife in the marriage union.

Why are gender roles so important in marriage? For one, God designed marriage, and when people do not follow his design, the marriage is destined for problems. It is important for us to know and follow his design, even when it is countercultural or contrary to what we are accustomed to.

We can discern the importance of gender roles by considering the first marriage in the Garden of Eden. Gender roles was essentially the first thing Satan attacked leading to the Fall. By tempting Eve instead of Adam, Satan was manipulating her to usurp the authority God had established. The Fall happened when Adam followed Eve who was deceived by Satan (Genesis 3:1-6).

God's original intention was for the husband to lead the marriage, which can be clearly discerned from Scripture. In this lesson, we will establish the husband's authority by looking at the creation narrative. We will consider the perversion of gender roles as a result of the Fall, and then we will consider God's reestablishment of the husband's and wife's roles by looking at other key Scripture passages.

Let's first start with a biblical foundation for male leadership. How do we see this established in the creation story?

God Created Adam Before Eve to Demonstrate His Authority

In the creation story, God first made Adam and then Eve as his helper. Genesis 2:18 says, "The LORD God said, 'It is not good for the man to be alone. I will make a helper suitable for him.'"

In 1 Timothy 2, Paul used the creation order as evidence for men being the leaders/teachers in the church and not women. Look at what he said in 1 Timothy 2:12-13: "I do not permit a woman to teach or to have authority over a man; she must be silent. For Adam was formed first, then Eve."

Some have tried to explain away Paul's teaching on male leadership in the church as simply cultural and, therefore, not applicable to the church today. However, Paul's argument for male leadership was not just a cultural argument. Paul used a creation argument for the establishment of male leadership, meaning that God established this order from the beginning. Certainly, in the ancient culture, birth order was very important. The first born child would often receive a double portion of the inheritance. Birth order showed one's rank. Similarly, Paul said God's creation of Adam first was not haphazard but by sovereign design. It was meant to show his leadership in relation to his wife.

God established the husband's authority in the home from the beginning of creation, and Paul's argument was that this authority should continue to be reflected in God's church.

In what other ways do we see the husband's authority reflected in the creation story?

Adam's Naming of His Wife Demonstrated His Authority

Another evidence of God's original design for male leadership in the home is demonstrated in the fact that Adam named his wife. We see Adam's naming of his wife in two parts. First, in Genesis 2, God called for Adam to name all the animals. After naming them, God caused Adam to fall into a deep sleep, and, from his body, God created Adam's wife. Then Adam immediately named her. Genesis 2:23 says, "The man said, 'This is now bone of my bones and flesh of my flesh; she shall be called "woman," for she was taken out of man.'" As Adam originally named the animals, he then named his wife "woman." Secondly, after the Fall, he then called her "Eve" because she would be the mother of all the living (Gen 3:20).

Similar to ancient times, naming in our culture still is a reflection of one's authority. Parents name their children since they are the authority. God's design for Adam to lead his wife can be clearly discerned from the creation story, both in the creation order and in the naming of his wife.

Gender Roles Were Perverted in the Fall

In the Fall, Satan tempted Eve to eat from the forbidden tree. Scripture actually says that Eve was deceived but not Adam. First Timothy 2:14 says, "Adam was not the one deceived; it was the woman who was deceived and became a sinner." Why does it say that Adam was not deceived but the woman was?

Remember, in the context of 1 Timothy 2, Paul is making the argument that women should not be the leaders/teachers in the church (cf. 2:12). He seems to be making the argument that the Fall happened because Adam willingly followed his wife instead of being the leader God had called him to be. Eve was deceived, and Adam followed even though he knew it was wrong. Satan's temptation disrupted God's original order.

With that said, let's consider the effects of the Fall on gender roles in marriage. God said this about the effects, "To the woman he said, 'I will greatly increase your pains in childbearing; with pain you will give birth to children. Your desire will be for your husband, and he will rule over you'" (Gen 3:16).

What did God mean when he said to the woman, "Your desire will be for your husband, and he will rule over you"? The meaning is ambiguous, but it is made clearer by considering the use of the Hebrew word "desire" in other texts

In Genesis 4:7, God used the same word to describe "sin" trying to dominate Cain and provoke him to anger over God's acceptance of Abel's offering. Listen to what God said to Cain:

Then the LORD said to Cain, 'Why are you angry? Why is your face downcast? If you do what is right, will you not be accepted? But if you do not do what is right, sin is crouching at your door; it desires to have you, but you must master it.'

Here the word "desire" means to control, and thus, we can understand the effect of sin on the distinct roles of the husband and wife (or man and woman). The wife would try to control the husband, and the husband would try to dominate the wife. The battle of the sexes was one of the results of the Fall.

We have seen these effects throughout history in many ways. In some cultures, the husbands are apathetic, spiritually lazy, and sometimes absent, consequently the wife has to lead the home. In others, the husband tries to dominate by force and the woman has very few rights. The domination of the male has been seen in the fight for women's rights throughout history. Many societies abuse women and treat them like a piece of property. This was never God's original design. This came as a result of sin—the man would try to rule the woman by force.

We certainly see the effects of sin in the dating realm. It is displayed in the predatory male who wants to dominate and sleep with as many women as possible. It is also displayed in the predatory female who seeks to control men with her beauty and use them to attain all of her desires.

Most importantly, we see this battle in the home, where the husband and wife strive for power—marring God's original design. God is a God of order; he understood that the institution of marriage could not function properly if it did not have clear leadership. This is true with any institution: the military, business, school, and even church. Therefore, God intended for the husband to be the leader in order to achieve his original purposes through marriage.

Obviously, this teaching is controversial. People seem to believe order and leadership in marriage means inequality. However, this is not true. A general and a private are equal in person but not equal in rank. Rank is needed to bring about good order and discipline in the military. Leadership is needed to accomplish the mission without discord. Similarly, God has a great mission for every marriage. It is the basic unit of all society, and when it is out of order, all of society is out of order. Therefore, he established clear leadership for this purpose.

Now, with that said, what should the husband's leadership look like practically? What should the wife's submission look like? The husband is not supposed to be a dominate tyrant and the wife is not called to be a doormat. In the beginning, God called Adam and Eve to rule and steward creation together. This loving and orderly partnership was meant to accomplish God's mission on the earth.

What should the husband's and wife's roles look like in marriage? Personality and upbringing make each godly home different, but the basic roles and principles should be the same.

The Husband Must Love His Wife

Instead of using his leadership to control or dominate his wife, God calls the husband to use his leadership to love his wife. God planned this from the beginning. The husband would lead through loving his wife. What should this love look like? Paul teaches that the husband's love should mirror Christ's love for the church. In Ephesians 5:25-28, he says:

> Husbands, love your wives, just as Christ loved the church and gave himself up for her to make her holy, cleansing her by the washing with water through the word, and to present her to himself as a radiant church, without stain or wrinkle or any other blemish, but holy and blameless. In this same way, husbands ought to love their wives as their own bodies. He who loves his wife loves himself.

What can we learn about a husband's love from Christ's example?[1]

1. The husband's love must *be realistic.*

The husband should have no fantasies about the woman he is marrying (v. 25). Christ loved the church, but he knew she was sinful and disobedient. Christ gave his life for the church while knowing her faults. His love was realistic.

In marriage, both mates must grasp this reality. In fact, much of pre-marital counseling is destroying the false expectations set up through romantic comedies and Hollywood. The husband must love realistically. This woman does not walk on water; she has been infected by sin just as he has. She must be reformed daily by God's grace, and she must be loved through her faults. Scripture says, "Love covers a multitude of sins" (1 Peter 4:8). Having a realistic love is important for both mates because if they don't have it, they will become disillusioned. No doubt, one of the reasons for such a high number of divorces in the first year of marriage is because most love is not realistic.

2. The husband's love must *be sacrificial.*

He is to love her as Christ loved the church and be willing to die for her (v. 25). It should be understood that if anybody feels like the wife's role is unfair, they

26

should give more thought to the man's. It is much easier to submit to someone than to give one's life for that person. This love that the husband is supposed to embody is impossible apart from the grace of God. To love sacrificially means the husband must often give up other things in order to serve and please his wife. He must sacrifice for her. He must sacrifice time, friendships, career, entertainment, hobbies, etc., in order to love his wife like Christ.

3.   The husband's love must *be purposeful.*

The purpose of Christ's love is to make the church holy, cleansing her by washing with the Word (v. 26-27). Christ's purpose is to make the church a perfect bride. Similarly, the husband must love his wife through teaching her Scripture, getting her involved in a Bible preaching church, and encouraging her to get involved with the ministries of the church.

He must seek to cultivate not only her character but also her calling, so she can fulfill God's plans for her life. He must help her discern her gifts and talents and encourage her in the use of them for the glory of God. This purposeful love also means at times admonishing her to help her know Christ more. Every man should consider if he is ready and willing to love a woman in this way even before getting married. Is he ready to be a spiritual leader? Is he ready to be devoted to the spiritual development of his wife?

4.   The husband's love must *be personal.*

He must love her as his own body (v. 28). Every day the husband brushes his teeth, combs his hair, and clothes himself. Every day he maintains his body. Sadly, husbands often go weeks without ministering to their wives. It is very easy to get so busy with life, work, and ministry that one inadvertently allows weeds to grow in his marriage. Love must be personal. He must love her like his own body. He must daily take time to cultivate a happy home.

When the world hears the phrase "male leadership," it often has negative connotations, but it should not if properly understood. Consider what Christ taught his disciples about leadership in Luke 22:25-27.

> Jesus said to them, 'The kings of the Gentiles lord it over them; and those who exercise authority over them call themselves Benefactors. But you are not to be like that. Instead, the greatest among you should be like the youngest, and the one who rules like the one who serves. For who is greater, the one who is at the table or the one who serves? Is it not the one who is at the table? But I am among you as one who serves.'

As described in Luke 22, male leadership primarily means greater service. Christ told his disciples that whoever wanted to be the greatest must be like "the youngest." The Jewish culture was very hierarchical, meaning that the youngest would always serve the oldest. But, Jesus spoke to this hierarchical culture and said that true leadership is servant leadership. To lead means to be like the youngest—the servant of all. True leaders will forego their right of being served in order to serve others. That's how husbands should be in marriage. They should be constantly humbling themselves in order to serve their wives.

Christ demonstrated this leadership in John 13, when he did the work of a slave by washing his disciples' feet. There is nothing negative about this type of leadership. God always intended this type of loving leadership for the marriage relationship, and the husband must daily seek to cultivate it.

What other traits should characterize gender roles in marriage?

The Husband Must Submit to Christ's Leadership

First Corinthians 11:3 says: "Now I want you to realize that the head of every man is Christ, and the head of the woman is man, and the head of Christ is God."

In this verse, we see the divine prerogative: Christ submits to God, the man submits to Christ, and the woman submits to man. If the husband is going to lead his wife according to God's design, he must first submit to Christ. It is for this reason that a wife must submit to her husband, for when she is following her husband, she is really submitting to Christ's delegated authority.

This brings a grave responsibility to each husband to know Christ's leading. He must truly be somebody who abides in God's Word and prayer so that he can discern God's voice. The man considering marriage should ask himself, "Am I pursuing the Lord in such a way that I can know his voice in order to lovingly lead a wife and a family?" It has commonly been said, "Only those who are near, hear." The husband must be near Christ, his head, to hear his voice. Only the husband who is near Christ will be able to model Christ and lead properly.

This is also important for single women to hear and consider because not every man is spiritually fit for leadership. They should ask themselves about a potential husband, "Does this man love Christ? Is this man following Christ? Is he spiritually fit to lead?" One can be sure that if a single man is not faithful in following Christ, he will not be faithful when married. Scripture says that he who is unfaithful with little, will be unfaithful with much (Luke 16:10, paraphrase). Husbands must continually be submitting to the leadership of Christ in order to properly lead their homes.

The Wife Must Submit to Her Husband's Leadership

As mentioned previously, in submission to Christ, the wife must submit to her husband. Ephesians 5:22 says, "Wives, submit to your husbands as to the Lord."

Scripture commands the wife to submit to her husband as though she were following Christ. The word "submit" is a military word that means to "come up under." Like a sergeant submitting to a colonel, the wife must submit to her

28

husband in every area, unless it would cause her to disobey her Commander and Chief, Christ. In every decision, the woman must obey her husband, unless his leadership is leading her to sin. In military terminology, this would be called an "unlawful order." The wife must wisely discern this.

With that said, this certainly does not exclude the wife's ability to make decisions on her own. Christ in leading us gives us many responsibilities and a form of autonomy under his authority. In following Christ, he often does not tell us to go to the left or to the right or when to rest. Scripture calls for us to be wise people and use the principles given in Scripture. Similarly, the wife may have many areas of leadership under her husband's authority.

For some, the wife will be autonomous in the area of caring for the home, even though she is still under her husband's leadership. For others, the wife will oversee finances. Good leaders recognize others' strengths and lean on them in those areas. This will be true in every marriage, and it may look a little different in every marriage.

This may be a revolutionary concept that a newly married woman must come to grips with. No longer is it simply, "Am I honoring the Lord in my actions and endeavors?", but also "Am I honoring my husband, who the Lord has called me to follow?"

Consider the honor given to Sarah because of the way she submitted to her husband, Abraham. First Peter 3:5-6 says this:

> For this is the way the holy women of the past who put their hope in God used to make themselves beautiful. They were submissive to their own husbands, like Sarah, who obeyed Abraham and called him her master. You are her daughters if you do what is right and do not give way to fear.

Sarah called her husband master, and Scripture says this is one of the characteristics that makes a woman beautiful to the Lord. A female considering marriage must ask herself, "Am I ready to honor and submit to my husband as unto the Lord? Am I willing to submit to his plans as he hears from God?" The one who is not willing to submit should consider if she is really ready to be married.

The Wife Must Submit to Christ's Leadership

Again, Ephesians 5:22 says, "Wives, submit to your husbands as to the Lord." Not only does this teach that wives must submit to their husbands, but the implication is that they must first submit to the Lord. The husband is just a representation of Christ's leadership, no matter how frail that representation may be. It is in submitting to Christ, abiding in his Word, and loving him that the wife will find the ability to submit to her husband. This will be especially true in dealing with a husband who doesn't know the Lord or who is far from him. First Peter 3:1-2 says this:

Wives, in the same way be submissive to your husbands so that, if any of them do not believe the word, they may be won over without words by the behavior of their wives, when they see the purity and reverence of your lives.

The husband's leadership applies even when he isn't following God. In that case, the wife's submission to Christ is even more important. By submitting to Christ, she will find ability to love and submit to a difficult husband and this submission may bring transformation and even salvation to his life. However, this is only possible when the wife is submitting to the Lord. Jesus said in John 15:5, "Abide in me and you will produce much fruit" (paraphrase). The ability to love, to have peace, to have patience, to forgive, etc., all comes from God.

The single woman considering marriage must ask herself, "Am I daily submitting to the Lord's leadership so I can faithfully submit to my husband's leadership?" This daily submission to the Lord prepares a woman for marriage.

Also, the single man considering marrying a female must ask, "How is her submission? Does she faithfully submit to the Lord? Is she faithful in church attendance, daily devotion, and service to God?" For if she does not submit to the greater, the Lord, then she will not submit to the lesser, her husband. A wise man will consider a woman's obedience to God when seeking a wife. God has called for the wife to first submit to Christ so she can faithfully respect and submit to her husband.

The Husband and Wife Must Train Their Children Together

Ephesians 6:4 says, "Fathers, do not exasperate your children; instead, bring them up in the training and instruction of the Lord." "Fathers" can also be translated "parents" (cf. Aramaic Bible in Plain English).

This means that both parents must work together to train the child and not exasperate him—leading him to rebel by dominant, loose, or unfair leadership. Parents must demonstrate godly leadership that models Christ, teaches the children God's Word, and draws them to a closer relationship with the Lord.

This is an impossible task for one parent alone and that is why God has given spiritual responsibility to both. The husband should still ultimately oversee this training, but the responsibility is shared. For that reason, parents must come to an agreement on how to train the child. If there is no unity in the training, it will have hazardous effects on the child.

Godly couples must sit down and discuss how this will be done. This will include discipline, spiritual training, academic training, athletic training, and areas of service, among other things. For spiritual training, many parents have given themselves to child catechisms, Bible memory, daily family devotions, as well as involvement in a Bible preaching church.

Sadly, what has happened in many Christian homes is that this call for the parents to train their children has been left to the church, the school, the grandparents, the babysitter, the athletic coach, etc. God never intended for these other mediums to raise the children exclusively; they should be supplements at best. Consequently, 75% of Christian youth fall away from God when they get to college because many parents have neglected their responsibility.

Engaged couples should consider their future children's training before they are married, since raising godly seed is one of God's primary desires for the marriage union (cf. Mal 1:15). Have you given consideration to how you will train your children?

Conclusion

The Fall corrupted God's original design for the husband and the wife. Because of sin, the husband naturally has a tendency to try to dominate his wife or to become a doormat for his wife. The tendency for the wife is the same. However, God's plan is for the husband to love and serve his wife and for the wife to submit to him. They both have a responsibility to raise the children in the admonition of the Lord. But, ultimately, the husband will be held accountable to God for his leadership or lack of leadership over his family.

Gender Roles Homework

Answer the questions, then discuss together.

1. What was new or stood out to you in this session? In what ways were you challenged or encouraged? Were there any points/thoughts that you did not agree with?

2. Often when beginning a marriage, spouses bring in different unspoken expectations. These frequently become points of discouragement and tension in the relationship. Discussing expectations beforehand will aid in making a smooth transition into marriage.

    What were the gender roles in your home? What role did your father fulfill in family devotions, discipline of children, finances, yard work, cleaning the house, etc.? What role did your mother fulfill?

3. List twenty expectations for your spouse in marriage such as: Who will do the house chores? What is your expectation for your spouse as far as spiritual devotion? What is your expectation for your spouse in the clothing he or she wears? What will you do for holidays? What side of the family will you spend Christmas, Thanksgiving, etc., with? How do you expect money and major decisions to be handled? Who will discipline the children?

4. Write down ten expectations that you think your spouse will have for you.

5. Discuss these with your mate and come to an agreement on the expectations that you will each fulfill. List the expectations that you have agreed on. Write them with this form,

    "I will commit to _____ in our marriage with the support of my wife/husband and by the grace of God."

6. After completing this session, in what ways do you feel God is calling you to pray for your future marriage? Spend some time praying.

Foundation Three: Commitment in Marriage

Many marriages were destined for trouble from the utterance of the words "I do." When the couple publicly declared, "I do", they really didn't understand what they were committing to. They had no comprehension of what true commitment was. They entered marriage thinking that divorce was a viable option in their pursuit of self-fulfillment and happiness, or they naively thought that it could never happen to them. For many there isn't much difference between their commitment in dating and their commitment in marriage. Marriage is just another way to express how much they love someone.

In many cultures, including the biblical culture, they practice arranged marriages, which typically has a very low divorce rate. In those cultures, "love" is more than just feelings; it means commitment. Love as a feeling will have seasons of strength and seasons where it seems to diminish totally. Marriages based primarily on one's feelings will have the consistency of the ocean during a lunar eclipse. This is why you often hear people say, "We just fell out of love," when divorcing, which means they lost the early feelings they had in the marriage.

In this session, we will consider love as a form of commitment. My favorite definition of love is "to give not caring what one gets in return." Many would call this love, agape, the Greek term for God's love for us. To agape means a married person is saying to his or her mate, "If at some point I don't have loving feelings for you, I will still love you. If you get sick and can't respond in love towards me, I will still love you. If you treat me unlovingly, I will still respond in love towards you." This type of love is divine, and it is this love God originally meant to be experienced in marriages.

God's Covenant Faithfulness with Abraham

In considering love as a commitment, let's look at God as an example of one in a committed loving relationship. We will see this in God's covenant with Abraham in Genesis 15. Genesis 15:7-21 says:

> He also said to him, 'I am the LORD, who brought you out of Ur of the Chaldeans to give you this land to take possession of it.' But Abram said, 'O Sovereign LORD, how can I know that I will gain possession of it?' So the LORD said to him, 'Bring me a heifer, a goat and a ram, each three years old, along with a dove and a young pigeon.' Abram brought all these

35

to him, cut them in two and arranged the halves opposite each other; the birds, however, he did not cut in half. Then birds of prey came down on the carcasses, but Abram drove them away. As the sun was setting, Abram fell into a deep sleep, and a thick and dreadful darkness came over him. Then the LORD said to him, 'Know for certain that your descendants will be strangers in a country not their own, and they will be enslaved and mistreated four hundred years. But I will punish the nation they serve as slaves, and afterward they will come out with great possessions. You, however, will go to your fathers in peace and be buried at a good old age. In the fourth generation your descendants will come back here, for the sin of the Amorites has not yet reached its full measure.' When the sun had set and darkness had fallen, a smoking firepot with a blazing torch appeared and passed between the pieces. On that day the LORD made a covenant with Abram and said, 'To your descendants I give this land, from the river of Egypt to the great river, the Euphrates."

Do you know anything about a blood covenant? A covenant is simply a binding agreement between two or more people. But, often in ancient times, they would seal the covenant in blood. In fact, the word "covenant" really means "to cut". They would take a few animals, most likely cattle and birds, and cut them in half. One person would walk through the sliced pieces essentially saying, "Let this happen to me if I break this covenant." Then the others would do the same.

In this story, God promised to give Abraham and his descendants the land of Canaan. Abraham replied to God in verse 8, "How can I know that I will gain possession of it?" God responded by initiating a blood covenant with Abraham. However, what makes this covenant interesting is that in verse 17 God walks through the pieces by himself without Abraham. He virtually said, "Let this happen to me if I don't fulfill this covenant." He put the ownership of completing the plan exclusively on himself, apart from Abraham's compliance.

As mentioned in session one, marriage was originally meant to be a reflection of God (cf. Gen 1:26-27). God made Adam and Eve in the image of himself. Yes, they were made in the image of God independently, but even more so together, as one flesh (Gen 2:24). Therefore, in marriage we are meant to reflect his love, his commitment. Scripture actually teaches that God is love (cf. 1 John 4:8), and though, we are not sovereign like God or holy like him, we are still called to imitate him in all relationships and especially in the marriage relationship (cf. Eph 5:22-33). Ephesians 5:1-2 says, "Be imitators of God, therefore, as dearly loved children and live a life of love, just as Christ loved us and gave himself up for us as a fragrant offering and sacrifice to God."

There is a sense in which we must have the same type of commitment with our mate that God had with Abraham. Abraham previously had committed to following God and fulfilling his will. In Genesis 12:1-3, Abraham left everything to follow God; he committed to God. But God's commitment to Abraham was unilateral, meaning God would fulfill his covenant even if Abraham failed. Similarly, in marriage we are saying, "I will do all that is in my power to love you when you fail me and to love you even if you don't love me. I will seek to love you as God has loved me. I am committed to you." No doubt, this is difficult. But this is how God loves us, and it is how we should love our spouses.

God's Covenant Faithfulness with Israel, Abraham's Seed

Another example of God's commitment to his people and what our commitment in marriage should look like is seen in the book of Hosea. God told the prophet Hosea to marry a woman who would eventually become a prostitute and cheat on him. God was going to use Hosea's marriage to display his commitment and love for Israel, who had been unfaithful to him by worshipping false gods. Look at Hosea 3:1-5:

> The LORD said to me, "Go, show your love to your wife again, though she is loved by another and is an adulteress. Love her as the LORD loves the Israelites, though they turn to other gods and love the sacred raisin cakes.' So I bought her for fifteen shekels of silver and about a homer and a lethek of barley. Then I told her, 'You are to live with me many days; you must not be a prostitute or be intimate with any man, and I will live with you.' For the Israelites will live many days without king or prince, without sacrifice or sacred stones, without ephod or idol. Afterward the Israelites will return and seek the LORD their God and David their king. They will come trembling to the LORD and to his blessings in the last days."

After Hosea's wife had left him and cheated on him, he sought to restore their relationship in obedience to God. While prostituting, she somehow became a slave. Hosea bought her out of slavery and took her back as his wife (v. 2). Hosea's love for his wife was meant to reflect God's love for the people of Israel. Israel had cheated on God, and yet the Lord still took them back, which reflects his committed love. Many theologians believe Israel's current state was prophesied by these verses. They are currently without priest, prophet, or sacrifice as they have rejected God. But when Christ returns, then they will be restored to God—their faithful covenant partner (v. 4-5).

Again, here we see God's covenant faithfulness. He will one day take his wife, Israel, back, even though she committed spiritual adultery. God covenanted with Abraham and his descendants, and he will be faithful to fulfill that covenant.

As Christians called to reflect God's image, we must seek to model his commitment to his people, his bride. It was this type of commitment that Hosea modeled in his marriage. He took his wife back, even though she cheated on him. By doing this, he modeled God's love and commitment to Israel. Marriage was always meant to symbolize God and his love for his people (cf. Eph. 5:22-27).

It is difficult to imagine a marriage partner being unfaithful or failing us in any way, but it is wise to consider your response to unfaithfulness even before entering the marriage covenant. If one of the purposes of marriage is to be a reflection of God's relationship to his people, then we cannot but consider this. As believers, marriage is not primarily for our self-fulfillment and happiness; it is to bring God glory as it reflects him.

In addition, we must consider this type of commitment because we are marrying people who are infected by sin and are prone to fail. If we are going to model God's love and commitment in marriage, we must ask ourselves, "Are we truly willing to be committed to our mates through the good and the bad, success and failure?"

In most marriages, couples are only committed when one person keeps his or her side of the covenant. However, that looks nothing like God's love. Marriage is different from dating. It is supposed to be a committed love, a persevering love, a hopeful love, especially when the relationship is tough. Again, one must ask himself even before getting married if he is really willing to display this type of commitment.

God Hates Divorce

As mentioned previously, arranged marriages have a very low divorce rate, and this may be true, in part, because of the great amount of shame that comes with divorce in those cultures. This is interesting to consider since there is very little to no shame for divorce in many other cultures, especially in the west. It has almost become popular. I read a bumper sticker the other day that said, "I am always right! Ask my two ex-wives." Divorce has become almost expected, which is why so many people are choosing not to marry and to instead just live together. And if they do marry, they realize that they have a "get out of jail" card, which they keep close to the chest.

This attitude is obviously very different from the way God views divorce. Consider God's anger over divorce in Malachi 2:16. It says:

> 'I hate divorce,' says the LORD God of Israel, 'and I hate a man's covering himself with violence as well as with his garment,' says the LORD Almighty. So guard yourself in your spirit, and do not break faith.

Here in this passage, God rebukes the Israelites because of how common divorce was in their culture. God said he hated the violence divorce created in the family, and he taught the Israelites to guard themselves and to not break faith with their wives.

Moreover, let's look at how Christ dealt with divorce in the New Testament. In Matthew 19:9, Christ says, "I tell you that anyone who divorces his wife, except for marital unfaithfulness, and marries another woman commits adultery."

In Matthew 19, Jesus gave one of two exceptions that can break the marriage covenant. The first is *adultery*. In a marriage where there is unfaithfulness, if the innocent spouse leaves the union, he or she is free to remarry. However, Christ said that if anyone married a divorced person, not under the exception of adultery, they would be living in a continual state of adultery. Why would they be in a continual state of adultery? This is because God still sees the divorced person as married to his or her first spouse. The first exception that can break the marriage covenant is adultery.

With that said, we must still remember God's ideal. Even though adultery breaks the marital covenant and allows the innocent spouse to seek divorce and remarriage, that still is not God's ideal. As seen in the book of Hosea, Israel was adulterous in their relationship to God many times, but he still continually took them back. As the prophet Hosea imitated God's committed love, he took his own adulterous wife back. Even under the exception, God's ideal is for the couple to restore the relationship, and by doing this, they demonstrate his committed love. Look at what Paul said about divorce in 1 Corinthians 7:10-11. He said:

> To the married I give this command (not I, but the Lord): A wife must not separate from her husband. But if she does, she must remain unmarried or else be reconciled to her husband. And a husband must not divorce his wife.

Those who get divorced, for any reason other than adultery, must remain unmarried or reconcile with their mate. This includes situations where there is abuse, irreconcilable differences, etc. *Marriage is supposed to be a life-long relationship, and when a person divorces, Scripture says he or she should remain single.*

In the case of divorce because of infidelity, the cheating spouse should be encouraged to seek reconciliation. If that is impossible, they must recognize that cheating is not an unforgivable sin. Jesus Christ died on the cross for all of our sins and there is forgiveness available (cf. 1 John 1:9). However, forgiveness does not always remove the consequences. If reconciliation is impossible, the cheating spouse must accept God's forgiveness and give himself to a life of serving the Lord as a single person. God will give him grace to fulfill that call and will make him fruitful, if he is faithful. As for the innocent spouse, God's ideal is for her to seek to restore the marriage. If that is not possible, she is free to marry another.

Why are we considering divorce and remarriage in a pre-marital/marital counseling study? It is because those who want to follow God's design must understand how important the marriage covenant is to God. For God, marriage is to be a committed relationship that is essentially unbreakable. Those who break it, except under adultery, are to stay single and continue to pursue the Lord.

These regulations for marriage are strict and were given by God to discourage divorce. In a society with no regulations and no shame with regards to divorce, it has become rampant and a viable option in a difficult marriage. Scripture teaches marriage is a covenant which should reflect God's covenant with us. Even when we fail him and turn our backs on him, he remains faithful because of his covenant which he sealed with the blood of his Son.

What is the second exception that would break the marriage covenant?

In Romans 7:1-3, Paul said this:

> Do you not know, brothers—for I am speaking to men who know the law—that the law has authority over a man only as long as he lives? For example, by law a married woman is bound to her husband as long as he is alive, but if her husband dies, she is released from the law of marriage. So then, if she marries another man while her husband is still alive, she is called an adulteress. But if her husband dies, she is released from that law and is not an adulteress, even though she marries another man.

Here, Paul taught that the second exception, which would allow for remarriage, is *death*. Death breaks the marriage covenant. Marriage is a physical covenant that makes a couple one flesh (Gen 2:24). They become one in body, soul, and spirit. Only a physical thing can break this covenant and that would be adultery or death. In fact, in the Old Testament a cheating spouse was put to death, and then, the faithful spouse was allowed to remarry (Lev. 20:10). In the New Testament, this is no longer true, but the cheating spouse is called to remain single.

Again, it should be heard that divorce is not an unforgivable sin. God's love and grace are experienced in an even greater way in our failures. Where sin increases, grace increases all the more (Rom 5:20). God certainly wants to give grace to restore divorced couples to one another and more importantly to himself. As the church, Christ's body, we must love and comfort those who suffered through a divorce. With the advent of sin, marriage has been severely damaged, and sadly, most, in some way or another, will be affected by divorce. But where there is sin and brokenness, we, as God's church, must seek to be conduits of God's abundant grace so there can be healing and restoration for all who suffered.

Doesn't the amount of commitment required for marriage, especially a bad marriage, sound scary? It almost sounds impossible. The marriage union is supposed to be a lifetime commitment, without a "get out of jail" card. It is meant to be something that can only be done through God's power. In fact, when the disciples heard of these rigid stipulations, they responded with a similar awe. They said, "If this is the situation between a husband and wife, it is better not to marry" (Matt 19:10). That's how strict the stipulations seemed to the disciples, and it should also challenge us as we consider this lifetime covenant.

Again, why do you think God made the marriage covenant so stringent?

40

Simply put, our God hates divorce, and he intended for people to marry and stay together forever. Our legal system provides strenuous consequences to discourage people from stealing, killing, raping, etc. Heinous crimes can incur a potential lifetime sentence in prison or the death penalty. Extreme consequences deter sin in society. This is the same thing God has done with marriage.

He wants people to know that marriage is a life-long calling. It is a covenant commitment and the only way out is to, essentially, remain single. Because people in the church have not been taught this or truly considered it, they have adopted the culture of the world, which looks at divorce as a viable option or as a necessary consequence of seeking self-fulfillment and happiness. If divorce is necessary to find happiness they say, then so be it. And, therefore it has become increasingly common even among Christians. Statistics reflect no difference in the number of divorces occurring in the church compared to those outside the church. However, since marriage is meant to reflect God and his love for his people, it is meant to be a union based on commitment. It is a union in which both say, "I will love you even when you are unlovable, and even when I don't feel like loving you. I will love you like God loves me for his glory and his fame which is my purpose in life."

Conclusion

Have you ever looked at marriage in light of this kind of commitment?

Just as God covenants with his people through the good, the bad, and the ugly, so must we consider marriage as a lifelong covenant. It is a covenant based on commitment and not feelings, for feelings come and go. We approach this covenant realizing the potential consequences of not fulfilling it, just as people did in establishing an ancient covenant. We must come into this covenant seeking to resemble and reflect God's covenant love for us.

How do you think understanding the realities of this sacred covenant should affect premarital couples or those already married?

Certainly, at the minimum, it should make couples re-evaluate their commitment. They should ask themselves, "Am I truly willing to love like God loves and commit like he commits for his glory and joy?"

Commitment in Marriage Homework

Answer the questions, then discuss together.

1. What was new or stood out to you in this session? In what ways were you challenged or encouraged? Were there any points/thoughts that you did not agree with?

2. What disciplines will you continually practice in order to help maintain your faithfulness and commitment in marriage? What steps would you take if you were having serious difficulties in marriage? How would you help restore your union? (Include who you will seek help from.)

3. Write down all the strengths of your mate which may aid having a committed and successful marriage.

4. Write down all the weaknesses of your mate which may hurt having a committed and successful marriage.

5. Write down all your strengths which may help having a committed and successful marriage.

6. Write down all your weaknesses which may hurt having a committed and successful marriage.

7. Discuss these with your mate. What *action steps* should you take as a couple to work on any weaknesses?

8. (If your mate is not willing to work on weaknesses, then you should discern how dangerous these weaknesses are, if they are something you can live with, or if his or her unwillingness to work on them may be a foreboding sign of not being willing to compromise in the future. This might be something worth talking more about together and/or bringing up with your pastor or mentor in order to further discuss and evaluate.)

9. After completing this session, in what ways do you feel God is calling you to pray for your future marriage? Spend some time praying.

Foundation Four: Communication in Marriage

At the core of every healthy marriage is the ability of a couple to successfully communicate with one another. Communication can be difficult because each individual may have a different background, experiences, and sometimes even culture, which all affect communication. In addition, 60 to 90% of all communication consists of body language, eye contact, facial expressions, and tone rather than words. Communication is a skill that must be learned and practiced in order to have a successful marriage.

The Bible teaches us a great deal about communication, since God, the author of the Bible, is a communicator. When he created the heavens and the earth, he did it by communicating. He said, "Let there be light." In fact, through nature he speaks to us every day. David said this:

> The heavens declare the glory of God; the skies proclaim the work of his hands. Day after day they pour forth speech; night after night they display knowledge. There is no speech or language where their voice is not heard. Their voice goes out into all the earth, their words to the ends of the world.
> Psalm 19:1-4

God speaks to us through nature, telling us of his great glory and splendor. He also speaks to us through his Son, who came to the earth not only to die for our sins but also to give us the Father's words. In fact, John the Baptist called Jesus "the Word" (John 1:1); he was the very communication of God. Jesus said this about his teaching: "My teaching is not my own. It comes from him who sent me" (John 7:16). And, ultimately God speaks to us through the Scriptures by the Holy Spirit (cf. 2 Tim 3:16-17). God is a communicator, and man, who is made in the image of God, is a communicator as well.

Proverbs 18:21 says, "The tongue has the power of life and death, and those who love it will eat its fruit."

What do you think Solomon meant when he said the power of life and death is in the tongue?

Solomon understood that as people made in the image of God, we similarly have power in our tongues. We have power to create and power to destroy. We can encourage people and lift them up with our words or destroy them with our words.

45

Whoever said, "Sticks and stones may break my bones, but words will never hurt me," was very mistaken. Many people carry great hurt and pain from words spoken over them years ago. They were ugly, skinny, fat, not smart enough, not athletic enough, not social enough, etc., and that stigma stayed with them for years. In the same token, people who have had encouraging friends, family, and community typically are confident and hopeful. In fact, words spoken over people can even affect their destiny. James, the brother of Jesus, taught that even though the tongue is a small member of the body, it controls the body. It guides the body like the bit in a horse's mouth or the rudder of a ship (cf. James 3:1-6). There is a tremendous power in our words to give life or bring death.

The power of communication is especially important in the context of marriage. By our words, we can develop a beautiful and prosperous marriage that glorifies God. And, by our words, we can destroy the very gift and mission God has given us in marriage.

In this session, we will consider principles that will enhance communication in marriage. We will study the importance of growing in knowledge of your mate, honoring and accepting gender differences, always speaking edifying words, listening to your mate, and learning to remain in Christ.

Know Your Mate

The first principle that will enhance communication is simply getting to know your mate. Peter said this in 1 Peter 3:7: "Husbands, in the same way be considerate as you live with your wives, and treat them with respect as the weaker partner and as heirs with you of the gracious gift of life, so that nothing will hinder your prayers." "Be considerate" can also be translated "dwell with them according to knowledge," as seen in the KJV.

What type of knowledge must the husband develop in his relationship with his wife in order to respect and honor her? The husband must develop knowledge of his wife's person. Each person is uniquely made. Things that bother the wife might not bother the husband. Things that excite the husband might not excite the wife and vice versa. There is often miscommunication in marriage simply because couples do not know each other well enough.

The husband must learn what makes the wife happy, what makes her sad, and what angers her and use this information to build her up and communicate with her better. Even though Peter speaks to husbands, this is certainly true for wives as well. In Greek, the word "know" typically refers to not just an intellectual knowledge but also an experiential knowledge. The husband and wife must know each other intimately so they can better communicate with one another.

How should they develop this knowledge? As Peter said, they develop it by spending time with one another (i.e. "dwell"). While dating, couples often spend as much time as possible with one another, but sadly in marriage, quality time starts to fade. The husband has work; the wife is caring for the house and children and possibly working as well. As the children get older, the husband and wife spend more time focusing on the children and less time on one another. As this rhythm continues, they eventually get to the point where they no longer know one another at all. These two individuals change every day and to continue to know one another intimately, they must make time for one another. This time could include yearly couple retreats, weekly date nights, and daily times of intimate communication. My wife and I try to spend at least the last hour of every day with one another, without the TV or computer on. By doing this, we aim to get to know one another better.

The more distant spouses become, the greater they struggle with communication. This is also true of pre-married couples. Courtship and engagement are very special seasons that help lay the foundation for future building. Couples who communicate well, know each other well. And those who don't know each other well, don't communicate well.

How is God calling you to strategically grow in intimacy with your mate?

Honor and Accept Gender Differences

The next principle necessary in marital communication is not only knowing your mate but accepting and honoring your mate as the man or the woman God made them to be. A common source of miscommunication in marriage is the simple fact that men and women are different. Not only does the opposite sex have many physical and emotional differences but communication differences as well, and these differences are often amplified in the marriage union. A great amount of fighting in marriage comes from not understanding and accepting these differences.

Many women grow up with a female best friend who they share all their feelings with, and in return, the best friend primarily gives affirmation. Men are typically more goal-oriented communicators. Communication is meant to accomplish something. Often male communication is used to decide where one is going, how to get there, and then what to do after getting there. It has a goal in mind. Whereas for a woman many times the goal is different. The goal could be as simple as expression, feeling heard and accepted.

Often women cry out, "Men!" And men cry out, "Women!" Both cry out in despair because they cannot figure out the other. The Bible teaches that God chose man and woman for one another. Eve was taken from Adam's ribs and formed perfectly to match him. Though different, man and woman were made for one another, and when unified in a godly marriage, there may be no greater way in which they demonstrate the image of God (cf. Gen 1:27).

In creating man and woman, we can be sure God was aware of the immense differences that could cause conflict in their relationship. Therefore, he gave clear instructions in his Word about how to navigate the communication gap in order to have a successful marriage.

Again, the apostle Peter, a married man, said this in his epistle:

> Husbands, in the same way be considerate as you live with your wives, *and treat them with respect as the weaker partner* and as heirs with you of the gracious gift of life, so that nothing will hinder your prayers.
> 1 Peter 3:7

Peter called wives the weaker partner (or weaker vessel) and commanded husbands to be considerate of them and to treat them with respect (or honor). What did he mean by the woman being the weaker vessel? Certainly, it means weaker physically, but it probably means much more than that. One interpretation is that weaker vessel has the connotation of more precious or more delicate vessel. Because the woman is more delicate than the man, he is more prone to hurt her physically, emotionally, and of course, verbally. For this reason, Paul commanded husbands to not be harsh with their wives (Col 3:19). Many times, the husband becomes harsh with his wife simply because of their differences—the different ways God made them. Therefore, Peter calls for husbands to not only be considerate of these differences but also to honor them (1 Peter 3:7). Though Peter speaks to the husband, the wife, certainly, must obey this as well. She must be considerate of her husband and the way God made him, and honor those differences.

As stated before, many men and women, instead of honoring the differences God created in the opposite sex, dishonor them and set out to change them. The man wants the woman to be more direct, to stop being so lady-like, and so sensitive. The woman wants the man to be more sensitive and to listen better. Certainly, there is much we can and should learn from the opposite sex. With that said, we must always "honor/respect" the unique differences that are rooted in how God created them. God made males and females different from one another.

Surely, as many married men do, Peter probably started out trying to make his wife more like himself. But Peter learned that God uniquely created women and those differences were to be honored. Therefore, this is an important principle to remember in marriage and one that God commends. Honor the unique characteristics of the vessel God created for you.

In my marriage, this has helped me tremendously. Where previously, I wanted my wife to change; I couldn't understand or accept her thinking. I've learned to accept and honor her as the more delicate vessel. God made her different from me, and praise God for those differences. Instead of trying to change her, I am learning to daily accept and honor her more. I want her to feel the acceptance and joy that God has for her uniqueness. In addition, I'm also learning how much I need each one of those unique differences.

Pre-married couples should learn to accept the differences in their mate, to honor those differences, and to learn from them. Since God made the woman to

48

help the man and the man to help the woman, they need to learn from one another. Learn how to honor those differences, and make your spouse feel accepted and honored for being who God has uniquely made him or her to be. This mutual honor will enhance communication.

Always Speak Edifying Words

Related to honoring our spouse, God makes it very clear that we should never dishonor him or her through our words. Watch any movie or TV show and you will see people disrespecting and dishonoring one another. Sadly, this often happens in marriages, in direct conflict with God's commands.

Paul says this in Ephesians 4:29-30:

> Do not let any unwholesome talk come out of your mouths, but only what is helpful for building others up according to their needs, that it may benefit those who listen. And do not grieve the Holy Spirit of God, with whom you were sealed for the day of redemption.

Through Paul, God commanded us to never let unwholesome talk come out of our mouths. This includes cursing, blaming, accusing, gossiping, lying, etc. All these are unfit for Christians to speak, especially in the context of marriage.

Paul also gives the positive directive of speaking "only" words that build the other up according to their needs (v. 29). In marriage, the majority of fights would never begin if couples spoke words that build up rather than tear down.

Psychologists have affirmed a useful method to aid in this process called using "I statements" instead of "you statements". When a wife says, "You never listen to me!" and "You don't care about me!" This automatically makes a husband feel attacked and go on the defensive.

Instead, it is suggested that we use "I statements" such as: "When you start talking before I finish sharing, I feel like you're not listening to me." "When you watch TV all night, I feel like you don't care about me." This is simply giving information, instead of accusing one of personal wrong. And, it opens the door for evaluating these feelings instead of fighting. This is a great tool that will help one speak only words that edify, especially when dealing with a potentially sensitive topic.

Practice the Art of Listening

In conjunction with speaking only words that edify, Scripture also gives us further teaching about healthy communication. James, the brother of Jesus, said, "My dear brothers, take note of this: Everyone should be quick to listen, slow to speak and slow to become angry" (James 1:19).

In order for a person to only speak edifying words, they must master the art of listening. Here are a few tips to aid in becoming a better listener. One should:

1.   Practice listening to what your spouse is saying.

It has often been said that God gave us two ears and one mouth so that we would listen twice as much as we talk. This is a wise principle in communication. We must practice listening.

Something that will help with this is practicing "active listening." We do this by repeating what our spouse said in order to get confirmation. For instance, one could say, "This is what I hear you saying, you feel neglected when I watch TV all night. Is that correct?" By repeating, you get to clarify your spouse's words and intentions. You also show him or her that you are trying to understand, which is important in communication.

2.   Practice listening to what your spouse is not saying.

Many times, there is more communicated by what a person is not saying than what is actually said. Communication is between 60 to 90% nonverbal. Sometimes, just the fact that a spouse is quiet may say a great deal. It may say he is not feeling well or he has more to talk about. This is something a good spouse will learn to discern. Study your spouse's body language and tendencies in order to enhance communication.

3.   Practice listening to the Holy Spirit.

God wants to give us wisdom to minister to the uniqueness of our spouse. He knows our spouse in a greater way than we do. Therefore, we should practice praying, even sometimes during conversations, so we can hear what God wants us to hear and say what he wants us to say (cf. Neh 2:4-5). James 1:5 says, "If any of you lacks wisdom, he should ask God, who gives generously to all without finding fault, and it will be given to him."

4.   Practice speaking less.

Of course, in order for a person to clearly listen to his spouse and God at the same time, he must learn how to talk less. Solomon said this in Proverbs, "In the multitude of words sin is not lacking" (10:19, NKJV). In many relationships, people talk way too much and, therefore, listen way too little, which leads to constant arguments. James said we should be quick to listen and "SLOW TO SPEAK."

Learn to Remain in Christ

As mentioned, Scripture gives us many principles about communication since our God is a communicator; however, with that said, one must realize that understanding these principles is obviously easier than putting them into practice. The Bible teaches that not only do we need God's wisdom but also God's power to communicate well because of our propensity to sin. Jesus said in John 15:5: "I am the vine; you are the branches. If a man remains in me and I in him, he will bear much fruit; apart from me you can do nothing."

These principles can only be successfully applied to a pre-marriage or marriage relationship if the people involved are walking closely with their Savior and abiding in his presence. When you remain in Christ, God will give you the fruits needed to be successful. These fruits include patience, self-control, love, forgiveness, and even the right words to say. Remaining in Christ is the secret to fruitful communication for both spouses.

How do we remain in Christ? Remaining in Christ includes, but is not limited to, disciplined prayer, Bible study, regular church attendance, serving, repentance of sin, and simply put, drawing near to Christ daily. By remaining in Christ, we recognize our inability to communicate well, and how, apart from his grace, we will destroy what God has given us. And for those who humble themselves daily before God, they will find great grace to communicate in marriage (cf. James 4:6, 10).

Conclusion

As we consider communication in marriage, we must remember God is a communicator and we are made in his image. Therefore, we are made to communicate. As we rely on God, through practicing principles in his Word, we can begin to use our communication to build our marriages instead of breaking them down. And, by his grace, we can start to realize his original plan for marriage—a union that brings glory to him and is a blessing to all.

Communication in Marriage Homework

Answer the questions, then discuss together.

1. What was new or stood out to you in this session? In what ways were you challenged or encouraged? Were there any points/thoughts that you did not agree with?

2. Peter said to dwell with your spouse according to knowledge (1 Peter 3:7, KJV). What intimate knowledge about your mate have you discovered that is especially helpful when communicating? What intimate knowledge about yourself would help your mate better communicate with you? How will you continue to cultivate this intimate knowledge in the marriage relationship, especially when life becomes busy with work, kids, ministry, etc.?

3. It is very common for couples to have communication problems in part because of gender differences and gender expectations. Are there any common miscommunication patterns in your relationship that may come in part from gender differences? How does a miscommunication often begin and what are its triggers?

4. What changes can be made on your side to better navigate these miscommunications? What spiritual or practical techniques will be used to enhance communication?

5. What ways have you experienced the importance of abiding in Christ for communication? How will you protect and cultivate an abiding relationship with Christ? How will you help protect and encourage this abiding relationship in your mate?

6. Write your parents a letter, an email, or give them a call to ask questions. Ask what positive attributes you possess that will help in marriage. Ask what negative attributes you possess that might hurt your marriage and find out how you can fix them. Ask for any pointers that will aid in achieving successful communication in marriage and a successful marriage in general.

7. Write your mate's parents a letter, an email, or call them and ask them questions. Ask what positive attributes does your mate possess that will help in marriage. Ask what negative attributes does your mate possess that might hurt your marriage and find out how you can fix them. Ask for any pointers that will aid in achieving successful communication in marriage and a successful marriage in general.

8. After completing this session, how do you feel God is calling you to pray for your marriage? Spend some time praying.

Foundation Five: Conflict Resolution in Marriage

How should couples resolve conflict in marriage?

Conflict is, essentially, part of human nature. After Adam sinned in the Garden, conflict ensued. When God asked him if he had eaten of the forbidden tree, he did not simply say, "Yes." He said, "The woman you gave me, gave me the fruit and I did eat." He indirectly blamed God and directly blamed the woman. The woman then blamed the serpent. When sin entered the world, so did conflict. In fact, God said that one of the results of sin would be conflict between the man and the woman. The wife would desire to control the husband and the husband would try to dominate the woman by force (Gen 3:16).

As we go throughout the biblical narrative, we continually see the fruit of sin displayed in conflict. In Genesis 4, Cain killed his brother Abel. In the same chapter, Cain's son, Lamech, killed another man and boasted about it. In Genesis 6, the world was full of "violence," and God decided to wipe out its inhabitants through the flood. However, the flood didn't change the nature of man, and therefore, conflict has continued throughout history. The world has known no time without war or conflict, and unfortunately, marriages are not exempt.

Paul taught that one of the fruits of the flesh, our sin nature, is "discord" (Gal 5:20). We are prone to offend others, to be offended, to hate, to withhold forgiveness, and to divide. Sadly, all these fruits are prone to blossom within the marriage union. Couples should be aware of this, and therefore, prepare to resolve conflict in marriage. How should couples resolve conflict in marriage?

In Conflict, We Must Have the Right Attitude

The first principle necessary to resolve conflict is to have the right attitude—one of joyful expectation in God. It is good to remember that conflict does not necessarily have to be detrimental to a marriage relationship. Conflict, as with all trials, is meant to test our faith, reveal sin in our hearts, develop character, and draw us closer to God (cf. Rom 5:3-5, Jam 1:2-4). Paul said this: "Not only so, but we also rejoice in our sufferings, because we know that suffering produces perseverance; perseverance, character; and character, hope" (Rom 5:3-4). Similarly, James said, "Consider it pure joy, my brothers, whenever you face trials of many kinds, because you know that the testing of your faith develops perseverance" (James

55

1:2-3). Paul said that we should rejoice in sufferings, and James said we should consider it "pure joy" when we encounter them because of God's purposes in them. God does not waste suffering, including conflict within marriage. God uses conflict to make us grow into the image of Christ (cf. Rom 8:28-29), which should be our ultimate goal.

Many times God uses our spouse as sand paper to smooth out areas in our life that don't reflect Christ. It has often been said, "Marriage is not about happiness; it is about holiness. And when we are holy, then we will truly be happy." In marriage, we enter the ultimate accountability relationship, which is meant to help us grow as God's children (cf. Eph 5:25-27).

Therefore, as James taught (James 1:2) and Paul taught (Rom 5:3), we should encounter marital conflict (and all trials) with joyful expectation, not because we enjoy suffering, but because we know God's purposes in it. We worship a God who took the worst sin that ever happened in the world, the murder of his Son, and made it the best thing. It is for this reason that we can have a joyful expectation, even in conflict. This isn't a denial of pain. It is both a recognition of pain and a future hope. It is like a mother giving birth. Even in the midst of pain, there is a joyful expectation. Many couples, who have gone through very difficult conflict, developed some of the strongest marriages—marriages used to counsel and repair others.

What is your attitude when you encounter conflict with your mate? If we don't have the right attitude, if we are angry at our mate and angry at God, if we are depressed, bitter, and disillusioned, then it will negatively affect our behavior and our spouse, and therefore, reap harmful consequences in marriage. Conflict is really just an opportunity to grow, and we should view it that way.

What is your attitude during conflict? Do you have a joyful expectation of the work that God wants to do? Do you expect him to make you holier? Do you expect him to strengthen your capacity to love? That's how Scripture tells us to view all trials.

In Conflict, We Must Develop Perseverance

In continuing with what Paul and James taught about trials, both taught that trials produce perseverance. Paul then said perseverance produces character and character hope (Rom 5:3-4). James said that we should "let perseverance finish its work so that we can become mature and complete, not lacking anything" (James 1:3-4, NIV 2011). In marital conflict, we must develop perseverance so we can produce the fruits God wants to cultivate in our marriage.

This is difficult because the natural response to trials and conflict is to bail or quit. And that's what many couples do. At some point they say, "That's enough; I can't live like this" and they quit. Some do this by divorcing, others by distancing themselves emotionally and physically, as they stop working to fix the marriage. However, Scripture teaches us to persevere in trials, which includes conflict. The word means to "bear up under a heavy weight." God matures us individually and corporately as we bear up under the heavy weight. He teaches us to trust him more. He helps us develop peace, patience, and joy, regardless of our circumstances. He helps us grow in character as we "let perseverance finish its work."

In order to resolve conflict, we must develop perseverance. That's essentially what we promised to do in our wedding vows. We committed to love our spouse in sickness and in health, for better or for worse. We should be thankful when it is "better" and persevere when it is "worse". For those who do, there is fruit. Paul said, "Let us not become weary in doing good, for at the proper time we will reap a harvest if we do not give up" (Galatians 6:9).

Do you feel like quitting? Hold on, because God has a harvest for you if you don't quit.

In Conflict, We Must Sow Good Seeds

Not only must we have the right attitude when encountering conflict, but we also must sow the right seeds to resolve it. Paul said that whatever we sow, we will also reap (Gal 6:7). Sowing and reaping is a principle God set throughout the earth, and it is at work within every marriage as well. If we sow negative seeds, we will reap negative fruit. It we sow positive seeds, we will reap positive fruit.

Sadly, even though we all want a positive harvest in our marriage, we typically respond in ways that are counter to that. A wife wants her husband to spend more time with her, but in order to get that, she criticizes him. The fruit she desires is opposite of the seed she is sowing. The seed of criticism will only produce a negative fruit in her husband. Similarly, a husband, who wants intimacy with his wife, actually begins to withdraw from her. He withdraws hoping that this will draw her closer, but it actually does the opposite. The negative seed of withdrawing cannot produce the positive fruit of intimacy.

In conflict, we must do the opposite of what our nature desires. We may have a desire to raise our voice, and/or to hurt the other person, but these seeds will only produce negative fruits and potentially destruction in the marriage. To resolve conflict, we must always sow the right seeds.

Similarly, consider what Paul taught about how we should respond to an enemy. He said:

Do not take revenge, my friends, but leave room for God's wrath, for it is written: "It is mine to avenge; I will repay," says the Lord. On the contrary: "If your enemy is hungry, feed him; if he is thirsty, give him something to drink. In doing this, you will heap burning coals on his head." Do not be overcome by evil, but overcome evil with good.
Romans 12:19-21

57

Paul taught that in response to an enemy, we must overcome evil with good. Instead of responding with anger or seeking revenge, we should sow kindness and generosity. If he is hungry, feed him. If he is thirsty, give him something to drink. Instead of being overcome by evil, we must overcome evil by continually sowing good.

What good seeds can we sow while we are in conflict? Maybe, it could be the good seed of a listening ear. It could be the seed of affirmation. It could be the seed of service. Certainly, it must be the seed of unconditional love. In conflict, we must sow good seeds to reap a good harvest.

With that said, we must always remember that conflict resolution is very much like farming. Sometimes, it may take months or years to get the harvest we desire. Many become discouraged while waiting for their spouse to change or for the conflict to be resolved. Typically, in that discouragement, people start to sow negative seeds that only hinder the harvest they seek. A verse worth repeating while considering conflict resolution is, "Let us not become weary in doing good, for at the proper time we will reap a harvest if we do not give up" (Galatians 6:9). We must not only sow good seeds, but we must faithfully do it until God brings the harvest. We plant and water, but only God makes the seed grow in his time (cf. 1 Cor 3:6-7).

What type of negative seeds do you have a tendency to sow when in conflict? How is God calling you to sow positive seeds to reap a positive harvest?

In Conflict, We Must Talk to Our Spouse First Before Others

Another important principle to apply in conflict is talking to our spouse first before talking to anybody else. This is a principle that Christ taught about dealing with sin in general. In Matthew 18:15 he said, "If your brother sins against you, go and show him his fault, just between the two of you. If he listens to you, you have won your brother over."

This is important for several reasons. First, it shows respect for our spouse. It is disrespectful to discuss a problem with our mom, our friend, or anybody else not first discussed with our spouse.   If our spouse finds out, it may actually cause more conflict. Secondly, every story has two sides, and those who are closest to us (such as family and friends) may not have the ability to give us unbiased counsel. Even for myself, as a pastoral counselor, I have to work really hard to not jump to conclusions after hearing only one side of the story. This does not mean that we shouldn't talk to those closest to us, we should, but only after trying to resolve it with our spouse first. And when we do talk to others, we should still respect and honor our spouse.

Christ taught that when somebody sins against us, we should go to that person first (Matt 18:15). Many couples increase their conflict by bringing others in without first seeking to resolve it with their spouse alone.

In Conflict, We Must Seek Wise Counselors

Though this point may seem like it contradicts the previous one, it doesn't. Christ taught that we should confront a person in sin one on one, and if they don't respond, then invite others into the process, including the church. Matthew 18:16-17 says this:

> But if he will not listen, take one or two others along, so that 'every matter may be established by the testimony of two or three witnesses.' If he refuses to listen to them, tell it to the church; and if he refuses to listen even to the church, treat him as you would a pagan or a tax collector.

Though this was originally spoken about a brother in sin, it certainly applies to sin or conflict within marriage. God made us part of the body of Christ, which includes our marriage. When a natural body is sick, it often results in fever. In a fever, the body simply recruits itself to bring healing. In the same way, a Christian marriage needs the body's help to stay healthy. Marriages should always operate as a part of the body of Christ, but in times of difficulty, they need the body's help even more.

For many, this is countercultural. While in serious conflict, many couples hesitate to invite anybody into their marriage to help. Pride keeps them from exposing themselves and getting the help they need. This is actually another result of the Fall. When Adam and Eve ate of the forbidden tree, they looked at one another, saw their nakedness, and hid. They then put on fig leaves. At the Fall, humanity lost its intended transparency. We hide from one another; we put on a fake smile even when things are bad. We hide behind our clothes, our houses, our jobs, and our hobbies. We are deathly afraid of people knowing us: our insecurities and our problems. We even hide from God, as Adam and Eve did.

However, in order to build the healthy marriage God meant for us, we must be willing to expose ourselves and seek help. In Matthew 18, Christ said that if approaching the person in sin does not work, we should bring one or two others for accountability. If that doesn't help, invite the church. And if that doesn't help, the church should lovingly discipline the erring mate. This is difficult, but if we are followers of Christ, we must trust he knows best. God wants to use other godly people to speak into our marriage and sharpen it as iron sharpens iron (Prov 27:17).

Who would you invite to help your marriage? They should be wise people who can understand you, and who are walking with Christ—preferably a married couple. Solomon said: "For lack of guidance a nation falls, but many advisers make victory sure" (Prov 11:14).

Every president or king selects a cabinet with many advisers. The cabinet advises the president on foreign policy, educational reform, health care, etc., and this multitude of counselors helps bring victory. In the same way, a marriage needs a multitude of counselors, especially when in conflict. Yes, a couple should try to resolve the problem together first, but after that, they should seek help.

This should be considered even before getting married. Who will be your "many advisers" that make victory sure? It could be your parents, a wise couple in the church, your pastor, your small group leader, etc. The selection of these wise counselors takes great wisdom because all counselors are not created equal. These counselors should primarily use the Bible, as Scripture is sufficient to train us in all righteousness. Second Timothy 3:16-17 says this:

> All Scripture is God-breathed and is useful for teaching, rebuking, correcting and training in righteousness, so that the man of God may be thoroughly equipped for every good work.

God's Word is useful to train and equip us for every good work, which includes marriage. Those who disregard Scripture, do it to their own peril and that of their marriage.

In finding counselors, ideally, the couple would agree on whom to approach. But at times when one mate doesn't want help, the other mate may still need to seek help in obedience to Christ's teaching in Matthew 18. This is how Christ intended his church to function. Not only should we depend on God, but we should depend on one another. The eye cannot say to the hand, "I don't need you" (1 Cor 12:21). By not using the body, we spiritually impoverish ourselves. Independent couples may spend their entire marriage spiritually sick, or even worse, the marriage may end in divorce.

Who are your wise counselors who help you achieve victory? Have you and your mate considered this question? Are you willing to allow the church to be involved in your marriage as Christ desires?

In Conflict, We Must Immediately Seek Resolution

Another important principle that must be applied in marriage is to seek to resolve conflict as soon as possible. Both mates should agree to this principle early in the relationship. Paul said in Ephesians 4:26-27: "In your anger do not sin: Do not let the sun go down while you are still angry, and do not give the devil a foothold."

Paul says to get rid of anger before the day is over, because if we don't, it will give Satan a foothold. What does this mean? "Foothold" is war terminology. It means that unforgiveness and anger will give Satan a door to continually attack a person or a relationship.

We learn more about this from the Parable of the Merciless Servant in Matthew 18:23-35. In this story, a servant owed his master a great amount of money, so he begged for mercy. The master forgave him the entire debt. However, this servant had a fellow servant who owed him a smaller debt. The servant with the debt pleaded for mercy, but the servant, who had been forgiven, instead threw

60

him in prison. When the master heard about this, he became very angry and tossed the servant, whom he had previously forgiven, into prison to be tortured by the jailors. Listen to what Christ said to his disciples about this parable: "This is how my heavenly Father will treat each of you unless you forgive your brother from your heart" (Matthew 18:35).

Christ said to the disciples that if they didn't forgive others from the heart, God would do the same to them. Who are these torturers? No doubt, they refer to Satan and his demons (cf. 1 Sam 16:14, 1 Cor 5:5, 1 Tim 1:20). This is the consequence for harboring anger and unforgiveness towards others. If God has forgiven us of every sin we committed and will commit, how can we justifiably hold grudges against others, especially our spouse? When we choose to hold anger and bitterness, God hands us over to the enemy for discipline.

For many couples, because of their disobedience to God in holding bitterness and anger, their marriage has become a playground for the enemy. He lies to them; he accuses them. He tempts them to go outside of the marriage, and he also may bring sickness and other types of consequences for their rebellion (cf. Lk 13:11-16, Job 2:4-7).

To make this situation even worse, Scripture says when we are walking in unforgiveness, God will not forgive us (Matt 6:15) and he won't hear our prayers. Peter called for husbands to be considerate of their wives and to treat them with respect so that nothing would hinder their prayers (1 Peter 3:7). A marriage where the mates hold bitterness and anger towards one another is a marriage where prayer is powerless, which opens a greater door for the enemy to attack and bring destruction.

When in conflict, we must seek resolution immediately. Certainly, we can't force somebody to forgive us or to desire to work things out. However, we can do as much as possible to live at peace with someone. Romans 12:18 says, "If it is possible, as far as it depends on you, live at peace with everyone."

Are you holding a grudge against your mate? How is God calling you to seek resolution?

In Conflict, We Must Be Willing to Sacrifice

Intrinsic to the Christian life is sacrifice. We follow a Savior who left heaven and all the worship offered to him there to come to earth as a servant and die for the sins of the world. True followers of Christ should be known by sacrifice. In fact, Christ said that one could not be his disciple without taking up his cross daily (Lk 9:23). This life of a sacrifice should be especially displayed when in conflict. Paul said this to the Philippian church who was struggling with an internal conflict (cf. Phil 4:1-3):

> Do nothing out of selfish ambition or vain conceit, but in humility consider others better than yourselves. Each of you should look not only to your

own interests, but also to the interests of others. Your attitude should be the same as that of Christ Jesus:
Philippians 2:3-5

In the context of a call to unity (cf. Phil 2:1-2), Paul said the Philippians should "do nothing out of selfish ambition". The primary reason couples struggle with discord is because of selfishness. One person wants this, while the other wants that. However, Paul said to do nothing out of selfish ambition. In conflict, one must ask, "Is this desire something God wants, as displayed in his Word, or is this my preference?" Most conflicts are over selfish preferences instead of over something that genuinely matters, such as loving God and loving others, the two greatest commandments (cf. Matt 22:36-40).

Instead of being driven by self, Paul said to "in humility" consider others better than ourselves and to seek the interest of others. In conflict, one must ask, "How can I seek my spouse's betterment or desires over mine?" Essentially, Paul was calling the Philippian church to live a life of sacrifice in order to be unified (v. 2). This sacrifice was further magnified when he said, "Your attitude should be the same as that of Christ Jesus" (v. 5). In the rest of the text, he described how Christ gave up his rights as God, took the form of a servant, died on the cross, and how God exalted him for his sacrifice (v. 6-9). This is the mind that should be in Christians, helping them to walk in unity with their brothers and sisters. And this is the mind that should be seen in every marriage, enabling them to walk in unity instead of discord (cf. Eph 5:25).

Christian couples should resolve their conflicts by caring more for their spouse's desires than their own. They should humble themselves even as Christ did. He gave up his comfort and his rights to serve us.

How is God calling you to sacrifice in order to resolve conflict or a potential conflict in marriage? Is he calling you to give up a friendship that is a bad influence or causes discord? Is he calling you to help more around the house, to care more for the kids, to start participating in something your spouse enjoys but you don't, to spend more time with your spouse instead of doing something else? How can you demonstrate Christ's sacrifice in your marriage? Sacrifice is the secret to resolving conflict, while selfishness is the catalyst of conflict.

In Conflict, We Must Love Our Spouse Deeply and Cover His or Her Sins

Finally, when in conflict, we must love our spouse and cover his or her sins. First Peter 4:8 says, "Above all, love each other deeply, because love covers over a multitude of sins." The Greek word for "deeply" is an athletic word used of muscles stretching or straining.

This is a rich word-picture of our love during conflict. In the same way a muscle must be strained and stretched to develop and become stronger, God often strengthens our love through conflict and difficulty with our spouse. Even though this stretching hurts, it actually results in a greater capacity to love. Therefore, couples, who deeply love and cover one another's sins while in conflict, gain the ability to love more deeply. Certainly, this must be an encouragement as we stretch our love to cover our spouse's sins while in conflict.

Stretching our love will often mean overlooking and forgetting the failures of our spouse. First Corinthians 13:5 says love "keeps no record of wrongs." God will call us to not even bring up some issues. While others, he will call us to firmly speak the truth in love (Eph 4:15) and work towards a resolution, especially when it involves sin.

How is God calling you to love your spouse deeply and cover his or her sins in order to resolve conflict?

Conclusion

Because sin became part of the human nature in the Fall, we are prone to conflict, even conflict with those we love most. For that reason, we must wisely prepare for conflict because it will happen in the marriage union. We can resolve conflict by:

1. Having the right attitude: one of joyful expectation, instead of wrong attitudes.
2. Developing perseverance instead of quitting physically or emotionally.
3. Sowing good seeds to produce a harvest of righteousness in our marriage.
4. Talking to our spouse first before talking with others.
5. Seeking wise counselors to help us navigate conflict.
6. Seeking to resolve conflict immediately to prevent opening a door for the devil.
7. Sacrificing our rights and desires for our spouse.
8. Loving our spouse deeply and covering his or her sin.

Conflict Resolution in Marriage Homework

Answer the questions, then discuss together.

1. What was new or stood out to you in this session? In what ways were you challenged or encouraged? Were there any points/thoughts that you did not agree with?

2. Most couples usually argue over similar topics. These are called "triggers". This might be when the woman shops, the man watches TV, somebody doesn't pick up after him or herself, etc.

    Write down all the common triggers for arguments in your relationship. Why do you think these triggers commonly cause you or your mate to get angry?

3. In the session, we talked about not sowing negative seeds. Which negative seeds do you typically sow when in conflict (i.e. withdrawal, criticizing, complaining, seeking revenge, seeking to win arguments, etc.)? What about your spouse? How have you seen these negative seeds produce negative fruit? How can you sow positive seeds instead to reap positive fruit?

4. Solomon said in the multitude of advisers there is victory (Prov 11:14). Who would you talk to as a couple if you were having marital problems? If you were to choose a mentor couple for your marriage (someone to ask questions, to talk to about problems or successes, or even meet with regularly), who would you choose?

*Read the "Friends of the Opposite Sex?" article and answer the following questions:

5. What are your thoughts about the Chaplain's warning to the sailors about relationships with the opposite sex?

6. How will you handle relationships with the opposite sex? What specific things will you do in order to protect your marriage from open doors?

7. Do you have any other thoughts or concerns about this issue?

8. After completing this session, how do you feel God is calling you to pray for your marriage? Spend some time praying.

Article: Friends of the Opposite Sex?

How will you handle friendships with the opposite sex in marriage? This seemingly unimportant issue can often cause great strain and conflict within a marriage.

This topic came up while I was working as a Navy Reserve chaplain at Great Lakes Navy Base. While there, I attended a two hour group pre-marital counseling session for sailors. The chaplain running the session asked the sailors this question, "How many of you have friends of the opposite sex?" The whole class raised their hands. The next question was, "How many of your fiancés have friends of the opposite sex?" The whole class raised their hands again. Finally, he said, "How many of you plan on keeping it that way?" Each of the sailors looked at each other trying to discern what the right answer was, but eventually, all of them raised their hands again.

The chaplain then began to describe a formula of how relationships develop and progress further than friendship. He said:

> I know there are people in here who think their fiancé was the only person in the world they could ever fall in love with. However, let me quickly burst that bubble for you. There is a formula for love, and it is pretty simple. It is having a person of the opposite sex + time together + intimate sharing. Those are the only three things needed for you to become seriously attracted to someone, and it potentially can happen with anyone.

> Those of you who plan to keep your friends of the opposite sex, I would highly discourage it. Do you think most people who end up having affairs, initially planned to cheat on their mates? No, many times it happens simply because the couple did not have a rational plan about how they were going to interact with the opposite sex. They began to have fights and then one spouse went to share their problems with a friend of the opposite sex. When this continually happened, it created vulnerability and intimacy, eventually leading to an affair. Or, one mate had a job that required travel while the other stayed home, partied, and hung out with the opposite sex when the mate was away. Again, this produced the simple formula of the opposite sex + time together + intimate sharing, leading to problems.

These are not uncommon scenarios; they happen all the time. To make it worse, throw alcohol into the picture. Then anything could happen. It only takes one drink to lower your inhibitions...

The topic of friendship with the opposite sex is a topic every couple should consider before getting married. Personally, my wife and I talked about this before marriage, and we both agreed it was very difficult, even as a single person, to have a close relationship with the opposite sex without someone's feelings eventually getting involved. Not impossible, but difficult.

How did we decide to handle it? As a pastor, I have to minister to females, but I am very careful about being alone with them unless it is necessary for confidentiality. When I am going to be alone with a female for an extended period of time, I always try to let my wife know and make sure she approves. If the counseling will be continuous, I will probably ask her to get involved.

In addition, before I got married, one of my best friends was a female, and to be honest, feelings sometimes got involved. However, we never went further than friendship. In marriage, it was very important to me for my wife to become close with this female if my friend was to remain a part of my life. By God's grace, my wife now has a closer friendship with her than I do. For me, this was the only way my friend and I could continue to have a close relationship. With that said, my relationship with this girl is not even close to where it was previously because now my wife gets all my intimate thoughts, fears, plans, and time alone. That intimacy is reserved for my wife alone. And, by God's grace, this close friend is now also married, and her intimate thoughts are reserved for her husband.

Consequently, this is a very important issue for couples to discuss and to create a plan for. When not properly addressed, it often becomes a source of conflict and tension within a marriage and sometimes it can be destructive. How will you handle relationships with the opposite sex?

Foundation Six: Raising Godly Children in Marriage

How do we raise godly children in marriage? One of the reasons God brings two people together in marriage is for the purpose of raising godly children, children who look like him. Malachi 2:15 says:

> Has not the LORD made them one? In flesh and spirit they are his. And why one? Because he was *seeking godly offspring*. So guard yourself in your spirit, and do not break faith with the wife of your youth.

But how is this accomplished? Obviously, the only perfect model of parenting is God the Father, and therefore, as we look at him and his Word, we can discern principles about raising godly children.

In Order to Raise Godly Children, Parents Must Model Godliness

In order to raise godly children, by necessity, parents must model godliness. Children often model the character of their parents. Listen to how Paul challenged Christians: "Be imitators of God, therefore, as dearly loved children and live a life of love, just as Christ loved us and gave himself up for us as a fragrant offering and sacrifice to God" (Ephesians 5:1-2). He called them to imitate God, their father, as dear children and to live a life of love. As a parent, God is loving, righteous, holy, etc., and therefore, his children will in some ways reflect his character.

Similarly, parents must be people of character if they are going to raise godly children. Children raised in a loving home, by parents with character, typically mimic the virtues demonstrated by their parents. In contrast, parents who are not around, who lack self-control in their speech or with their anger, etc., produce the same character in their children. They won't be able to cultivate righteousness in them. In fact, the hypocrisy will only lead them to rebel.

Consider how Paul challenged Timothy, the pastor of the church of Ephesus: "Watch your life and doctrine closely. Persevere in them, because if you do, you will save both yourself and your hearers" (1 Timothy 4:16). Paul told Timothy to be careful about his doctrine (what he taught) and his life (how he lived), because if he did, he would save those who listened to him. Essentially, it could be said this way, "Timothy, if what you say doesn't match your actions, you will destroy those who follow you." And it is the same for parents. Many parents destroy their children because they have a speech that doesn't match their actions. They tell their daughter, "Stop cursing" as expletives fly out of their mouth. They tell their son, "Control your anger!" as they scream at the top of their lungs. The dad tells the kids, "Stop fighting at school," though he fights with mom at home all the time. In the same way, when parents teach their children to evangelize, serve the church, or care for the poor, but never practice these, then the children likewise will not practice them as well.

Parents who don't model godliness will not be able to cultivate it in their children. And sadly for Christian parents, the consequences can be disastrous; many children fall away from God all together because of the hypocrisy seen in their homes. In order to raise godly children, parents must model godly character.

In Order to Raise Godly Children, Parents Must Train Their Children in God's Word

In order for parents to raise godly children, they must not only demonstrate godly character but also teach them Scripture. This is how God the Father develops godliness in us. Ephesians 5:26 describes how Christ washes the church with the water of the Word to make her blameless and holy. Parents must do the same with their children.

Consider what the father, presumably Solomon, said to his son in Proverbs 2:1-13:

> My son, if you accept my words and store up my commands within you, turning your ear to wisdom and applying your heart to understanding, and if you call out for insight and cry aloud for understanding, and if you look for it as for silver and search for it as for hidden treasure, then you will understand the fear of the LORD and find the knowledge of God. For the LORD gives wisdom, and from his mouth come knowledge and understanding. He holds victory in store for the upright, he is a shield to those whose walk is blameless, for he guards the course of the just and protects the way of his faithful ones. Then you will understand what is right and just and fair—every good path. For wisdom will enter your heart, and knowledge will be pleasant to your soul. Discretion will protect you, and understanding will guard you. Wisdom will save you from the ways of wicked men, from men whose words are perverse, who leave the straight paths to walk in dark ways...

The father told his son to turn his ear to wisdom, to call out for it, to cry aloud for it, to look for it as silver and hidden treasure, and if he did, he would understand the fear of the Lord and find the knowledge of God. This wisdom would enter his heart and be pleasant to him. It would protect him, guard him, and save him.

When the father calls for the son to seek after wisdom, this primarily refers to knowing and obeying God, as revealed through his Word. Fearing the Lord is called the beginning of wisdom (Prov 9:10). Throughout the Proverbs, this father sits with his son and teaches him the importance of wisdom. He trumpets the benefits of it and seeks to train his son in its ways, so he can be protected and guarded. This is how it should be with every parent. The way they train their children in wisdom (godliness) is by emphasizing the importance of Scripture, teaching their children to memorize it, to apply it, to know and to love God. This must be the daily endeavor of every parent as they aim to raise godly children. The Word of God must be the lifeline of the home.

This is exactly what Moses commanded Israel's parents in Deuteronomy 6:6-9. He said:

> These commandments that I give you today are to be upon your hearts. Impress them on your children. Talk about them when you sit at home and when you walk along the road, when you lie down and when you get up. Tie them as symbols on your hands and bind them on your foreheads. Write them on the doorframes of your houses and on your gates.

Parents were called to impress the Word of God upon the hearts of their children by talking about it at home, when they went walking, when they went to bed, and when they got up. They were to tie Scriptures on their hands and their heads and to write it on the doorframes of their homes and the gates.

Parents can apply these principles very literally. They should have times of morning and nightly devotions with their kids where they read the Word of God, discuss it, and pray. They should talk about God's Word when considering their child's behavior (or other children). They should talk about God's Word as they critique an inappropriate commercial or scene in a movie. Parents should wisely lead children to recognize sin, our need for the gospel—Christ's death and resurrection for man's sin, and ultimately genuine acceptance of Christ's lordship. As children mature and want to go here or there or do this or that, parents should encourage them to pray to God and seek his wisdom. Parents who are trying to raise godly children must saturate their home with the Bible, as well as practice the truths in it.

Some may call this sheltering, but it isn't. These kids are still called to be salt and light in the world—to be a blessing to it. However, they are not called to be part of the world. They should think differently because they have a different purpose, and this all starts with a home that is saturated with God's Word.

Are you willing to saturate your home with the Word of God? It is the Word of God that trains children and equips them for all righteousness (2 Tim 3:16-17).

In Order to Raise Godly Children, Parents Must Discipline Their Children

In order to raise godly children, parents must discipline them. The word "discipline" tends to have a negative connotation but it shouldn't. It is a rich word. It means: "training to act in accordance with rules", "activity, exercise, or regimen that develops or improves a skill", or "punishment inflicted by way of correction or training."[2]

Since God is the ultimate Father, we must consider how God disciplines us in order to discern how we should discipline our children. Hebrews 12:5-11 says this about God's discipline:

> And you have forgotten that word of encouragement that addresses you as sons: 'My son, do not make light of the Lord's discipline, and do not lose heart when he rebukes you, because the Lord disciplines those he loves, and he punishes everyone he accepts as a son.' Endure hardship as discipline; God is treating you as sons. For what son is not disciplined by his father? If you are not disciplined (and everyone undergoes discipline), then you are illegitimate children and not true sons. Moreover, we have all had human fathers who disciplined us and we respected them for it. How much more should we submit to the Father of our spirits and live! Our fathers disciplined us for a little while as they thought best; but God disciplines us for our good, that we may share in his holiness. No discipline seems pleasant at the time, but painful. Later on, however, it produces a harvest of righteousness and peace for those who have been trained by it.

Hebrews says that every father disciplines his children (v. 7). It is mentioned as an expectation. God disciplines his children and so should every parent. God disciplines through trials and various hardships he allows Christians to go through. Their purpose is holiness (v. 10). In the same way, good parenting disciplines the children for the purpose of "training" and making them righteous (v. 11).

It should be noticed that this passage does not distinguish between punishment for sin (punitive) and hard times that God uses to train us (non-punitive). The writer of Hebrews simply says, "Endure *hardship* as discipline, God is treating you as sons" (v. 7). The writer sees God in control of all hardship, whether that be hardship as a consequence of sin (punitive) or as a consequence of living in a world full of sin (non-punitive). Regardless, the sovereign God uses all hardship as discipline to train his children in holiness and to make them into the image of his Son (cf. Rom 8:28-29).

Non-Punitive Disciplines

Similarly, parents must initiate various non-punitive disciplines that will encourage holiness in their children. For example, my parents made me participate in sports when I was young, not only to gain broad experiences, but to develop character traits such as patience, team work, humility, etc. At other times, my mom would tell me I could not go outside until I had read a book for an hour. This discipline was implemented in order to help me learn to enjoy reading. In addition, I was given chores to learn how to work hard, to manage time, and to learn the value of a dollar, as I was given allowance. On other occasions, I would have to finish an endeavor I started, but did not like, simply to teach me endurance—to not quit when things were difficult.

In the same way, God brings (or allows) non-punitive disciplines in our lives not because we're in sin but for training, in order to make us holier. Sometimes, he puts us in waiting seasons to develop patience. Sometimes, he brings us through hardship, like Job, to develop perseverance and to know God in a more intimate way. The hardship isn't necessarily a consequence of sin; it is allowed in order to foster faith in God and godly character traits. Similarly, as parents, we must stretch our children through various disciplines to help them grow.

Parents should wisely introduce various forms of discipline to their children for the sake of character development. These may include disciplines like learning to play an instrument, playing a sport, completing chores, working a job, reading, etc. It should include disciplines such as limited time playing video games, being on the Internet, watching TV and movies, staying up late, and even eating healthy. As a pastor working with college students, I have watched students fail out of school because they played video games all day or watched movies all night. Discipline in these areas of life starts in the home. Parents who do not implement these types of disciplines may raise children with no discipline at all, which will eventually result in negative consequences in their lives.

Punitive Disciplines

As far as punitive discipline, the writer of Hebrews shares two techniques that God uses in Hebrews 12:6. These techniques are more clearly seen in the KJV. It says, "My son, despise not thou the chastening of the Lord, nor faint when thou art rebuked of him: For whom the Lord loveth he chasteneth, and scourgeth every son whom he receiveth." There is a clear heightening of severity with each discipline. Chastening is a form of communication used to correct, such as a rebuke. As a discipline for sin, God will rebuke us through his Word, maybe through a sermon or a friend, calling us to repent and do what is right. If rebuke does not work, God then brings punishment. He scourges believers, which refers to a whipping. A believer who is in sin will experience many difficulties brought for the purpose of correction. For example, when Jonah rebelled against God's words, the Lord brought a storm into his life that almost killed him. In 1 Corinthians 11, the members of the

Corinthian church experienced sickness, weariness, and even death for taking the Lord's Supper in an unworthy manner (v. 29-31).

Similarly, parents must develop a system of discipline that increases in severity, which includes corrective communication and punishment, to foster holiness in the life of their child. Scripture teaches that "Foolishness is bound in the heart of a child; but the rod of correction shall drive it far from him" (Prov 22:15). Foolishness in the Bible refers to disobedience to God and his Word. Psalm 14:1 says, "The fool says in his heart there is no God." Parents must understand that foolishness is bound up in the hearts of their children. Children are intrinsically wired to disobey God and his established authorities—they want their own way. If not disciplined, children will live a life of rebellion against God and all authority.

Proverbs 23:14 says this about disciplining a child: "Punish him with the rod and save his soul from death." What type of death is the Proverb talking about? No doubt, this refers to a potential early physical death, but it also refers to spiritual death—separation from God (cf. Rom 6:23). Disciplining our children prepares them to live a long life (cf. Ex 20:12) and to know and follow God, as they eventually accept the gospel and submit to Christ's Lordship. An undisciplined child will be prone to continue in foolishness and never follow Christ. Discipline is not only important for a child's earthly life but for his eternal destiny.

Wise parents realize this and work hard to "drive" foolishness far from their children through measured discipline (Prov 22:15). Parents should discipline their children, not because they have been inconvenienced or embarrassed, but because their children have disobeyed and dishonored God. They discipline them out of love. Proverbs 13:24 says, "He who spares the rod hates his son, but he who loves him is careful to discipline him." This endeavor takes hard work and perseverance. Because of its importance, it deserves strategic planning and a partnership between both parents.

The two aspects of punitive discipline God uses on us, as described in Hebrews, are communication (rebuke) and punishment (scourges). The first step in punitive discipline should be consistent, corrective communication. Parents must expose what the child did wrong, why it was wrong, and warn of consequences—both short term and long term. When the child continues in sin, parents should lovingly punish to deter from further sin, even as God does with us.

The secret to discipline is a healthy balance between corrective communication and punishment. When children are young, there should be less reasoning and more punishment so that they learn obedience. As they grow older, there should be more communication and less punishment. If parents don't teach them obedience through punishment when they are young, they won't respond to communication and reasoning when they are old. There is a small window for parents to ingrain obedience in children while they are young (Prov 22:6); when they are older, it will be much harder.

What types of punishment should parents use?

In Proverbs, we continually see the word "rod" used in reference to disciplining children, as previously quoted. Let's listen to a few of these verses again.

Do not withhold discipline from a child; if you punish him with the rod, he will not die. Punish him with the rod and save his soul from death.
Proverbs 23:13-14

He who spares the rod hates his son, but he who loves him is careful to discipline him.
Proverbs 13:24

The rod of correction imparts wisdom, but a child left to himself disgraces his mother.
Proverbs 29:15

When the writers of Proverbs use the word "rod", it seems to primarily refer to forms of corporal punishment. There are several evidences for this. First, corporal punishment was a typical discipline in ancient societies including that of Israel (cf. Deut 25:3). Second, the fact that it is repeated so many times in the Proverbs makes it unlikely for the rod to be merely symbolic. Third, some verses clearly refer to corporal punishment. For example, Proverbs 23:14 says, "If you strike him with the rod, you will save his soul from Sheol" (ESV).

Due to the deplorable amount of child abuse happening in societies, spankings are commonly looked down upon and even considered barbaric. However, physical abuse, or any kind of abuse for that matter, was never God's plan for training children. God teaches the rod should be an act of love (Prov 13:24). It is loving parents seeking to save their children from death (23:14).

How should punitive discipline (including spankings) be administered to children? Here are a few guidelines.

1. Discipline should never be given in anger.

Scripture says, "man's anger does not bring about the righteous life that God desires" (James 1:20). When parents yell at their children or spank them in anger, they are abusing them. It will not produce the righteous life that God desires in children. Parents should be calm and measured when disciplining a child.

2. Discipline should be equal to the sin.

In the Mosaic law, civil discipline had to be equal to the crime; it was to be "an eye for an eye, and a tooth for a tooth" (Ex 21:24). This is also true in disciplining children. Parents must wisely consider the consequences for each infraction. If discipline is unfair, it may result in rebellion.

In addition, when deciding the punishment, parents must discern the difference between childishness and foolishness. Small children are going to spill milk; that is childishness. But when they spill the milk, were they doing it to be rebellious? Foolishness should be punished, and childishness should be corrected.

3.   Discipline should be consistent.

When a parent continually tells their children, "If you do this, then I will discipline you when we get home," and the parent does nothing, then children learn that the parent doesn't always mean what he or she says, and therefore, they don't always have to obey. Also, if the parent doesn't discipline the child for turning on the TV when they should be sleeping, but then does the next time, it confuses the child. Discipline must be consistent. In addition, the giving of discipline should also be consistent between the parents. Parents must present a unified front; otherwise, it will promote manipulation from the child and cause discord within the marriage.

4.   Discipline should create intimacy instead of distance.

When a child is being disobedient to his parent, distance is created in the relationship. However, when the parent disciplines the child, it shouldn't create a greater distance—it should restore intimacy. This is how God's discipline functions with us. Sin separates us from God, but his discipline is meant to draw us back into intimacy. This is another reason why parents shouldn't discipline when angry or give unfair disciplines; it further alienates the child instead of drawing him closer.

In developing a system of punitive discipline for our children, like our heavenly Father, parents must consistently correct their children through communication. They must teach them what sin is and why it is wrong, especially from a biblical perspective. They must warn children so they can turn away from temptation. When children sin, parents must consistently punish them in order to train them to honor God.

Parents must implement both punitive and non-punitive disciplines in order to promote holiness in their children. Non-punitive disciplines are as simple as reading an hour a day, learning to play an instrument, playing a sport, having limited time on electronics, eating healthy, etc. These will promote virtues like teamwork, perseverance, self-control, and moderation which will bless them for the rest of their lives.

What types of discipline will you implement in the lives of your children to promote godly character in them?

In Order to Raise Godly Children, Parents Must Avoid Provoking Their Children to Anger

As we consider discipline, it is very important for parents to not discipline children in a way that provokes rebellion. Colossians 3:21 says, "Fathers, do not embitter your children, or they will become discouraged." In this text, Paul spoke to fathers and commanded them to not embitter their children lest they become discouraged or "lose heart," as translated in the NASB. This is not simply referring to a child getting upset, for this is inevitable. It has to do with a deep–rooted, settled anger that stays in this child and affects his character for the rest of his life. This anger will result in rebellion both towards the parents and towards God, and may keep them from ever becoming the righteous seed that God desires.

The word "father" can also be translated "parents" (cf. Hebrews 11:23). This sin is committed not only by fathers; it is also committed by mothers. It is possible for parents to embitter their children to the point where they rebel.

How do parents embitter their children? This can happen in many ways.

1. Parents embitter their children by not disciplining them.

This is one of the quickest ways to develop bitterness in children. Spoiled children are thankless and bitter. Because they get their way all the time, they are bitter whenever any authority does not give them what they want or when life becomes difficult. As mentioned, Proverbs 22:15 says, "Folly is bound up in the heart of a child, but the rod of discipline will drive it far from him" (Prov. 22:15). Parents embitter them by never driving the foolishness, the sin, out of their hearts through discipline.

2. Parents embitter their children by abusing them or giving improper discipline.

Abuse, either verbally or physically, sows seeds of anger or hatred in the hearts of children. The anger sown is hard to remove. Many times these children abuse others because of the anger in them.

However, we see this not only as a result of abuse but improper discipline as well. When a parent unwisely uses his anger, it trains his child to unwisely use his also. For example, the parent becomes angry and curses at him, criticizes him, or even harshly disciplines him. Even if the punishment is just, the improper use of anger trains the child. The child learns, "When I am angry it is OK to curse; it is OK to hit somebody; it is OK to go crazy." He never learns how to properly control his anger and, therefore, struggles with anger throughout his life.

3. Parents embitter their children by neglecting them.

Many children grow bitter because their parents are never around. Consequently, they lack love and affection causing them to grow bitter. Some parents neglect their children for work. They work long hours in order to achieve a certain amount of success, and this keeps them away from home. Ultimately, this hurts children both emotionally and spiritually.

Sadly, in our society many parents neglect their children by sending them away to extensive education or extracurricular programs. Many times these programs are meant to compensate for their lack of presence. It is not God's will for teachers, coaches, or babysitters to raise children. That is why he gave children to the parents. Certainly, these people should play a role, but it is important for parents to be the primary influence in the lives of their children. Parents must be careful not to neglect their children.

4.   Parents embitter their children by never encouraging them and showing them affection.

We saw this in the story of Martin Luther. He had a father who never encouraged him or showed him love. Listen to what commentator William Barclay said:

> It is one of the tragic facts of religious history that Martin Luther's father was so stern to him that, all his life, *Luther found it difficult to pray: 'Our Father.' The word father in his mind represented nothing but severity.* The duty of the parent is discipline, but it is also encouragement. *Luther himself said: 'Spare the rod and spoil the child. It is true. But beside the rod keep an apple to give him when he does well.*[3]

Healthy parents not only discipline their children but also reward them. Parents reward their children when they do well and discipline them when they do wrong. Children start to learn fairness by this balanced approach.

5.   Parents embitter their children by showing favoritism toward other siblings.

We get a good picture of this in the story of Jacob, the father of Joseph. Jacob gave Joseph the robe of many colors, showing special favor to this son above the other eleven. This embittered the older siblings against the father and also against Joseph. Later, they kidnapped and sold Joseph into slavery out of anger (Gen 37).

How often do siblings become embittered against one another because of unwise parenting? These children grow up disliking one another. "Mother always thought you were the prettiest!" "Dad always liked you because you were the smartest and the most athletic!" This happens all the time, as parents embitter their children by showing favoritism.

Training children is a delicate ministry and parents tend to lose balance. Some parents become permissive, leading them into anger and rebellion. Others become authoritarians, leading to the same. In our parenting, God has called us to not embitter our children. When we embitter them, we can't lead them to God, which was the very reason God gave them to us.

In Order to Raise Godly Children, Parents Must Know Their Children

Finally, in order to raise godly children, parents must know them. As with all the points, this is a reflection of how God develops godliness in us as his children. He knows us. Listen to what God said to Jeremiah when he called him to be a prophet to the nations: "Before I formed you in the womb *I knew you*, before you were born I set you apart; I appointed you as a prophet to the nations" (Jeremiah 1:5). God knew Jeremiah intimately. Similarly, David spoke of how God knew him in Psalm 139:1: "O LORD, you have *searched me and you know me.*" To search means to "examine thoroughly."[4] God had examined David thoroughly, he knew him.

Similarly, parents must know their children if they are going to raise them in godliness and lead them into God's plan for their lives. Proverbs 22:6 says, "Train a child in the way he should go, and when he is old he will not turn from it." "In the way he should go" can also be translated as "his way" or "his bend." The Amplified Bible translates it this way: "Train up a child in the way he should go [and in keeping with his individual gift or bent], and when he is old he will not depart from it." The word "way" comes from a Hebrew verb used of a bow launching an arrow.[5] When a person shoots an arrow, the tension must align with the natural bend in the bow or it will break. This is also true in raising children.

Some parents damage their children by trying to train them in a way God didn't wire them. They may do this by pushing their kids into the medical field, athletics, etc., even though the children show no aptitude or passion in those areas. God gives us children who are already uploaded with a unique and specific program like a computer. We can't use software uniquely made for an Apple with a PC. It's the same with children. Some will be wired towards the arts, technology, or serving ministries. It is the job of parents to get to know the way God wired them, so they can encourage them in those areas.

This can be difficult for parents, especially if their child's wiring doesn't fit their expectation or what might be considered successful in society. However, we are called to train a child according to his own way—according to his own bend (Prov 22:6)—not ours' or others'. Their "way" may not appeal to us, but ultimately, we are raising children for God and to fulfill his calling on their lives. Like Jeremiah, God knew them before they were in the womb (Jer 1:5). Like David, they are fearfully and wonderfully made (Psalm 139:14) and called for a specific work (Eph 2:10). It is the parent's job to help discern this work and to help the children fulfill it.

In order to know their children and the way they are wired, parents must spend quality time with them. Just like the husband and wife must spend time together to cultivate their marriage, parents should spend quality time with each child. This can become complicated as the number of children grows. Many parents maneuver this by planning weekly or monthly dates with each child. For instance, every Wednesday night will be daddy daughter date, or once a month mom and son will go to their favorite restaurant, etc. Parents must take time to be with their children, to listen to them, to study them, and to have fun with them, ultimately for the purpose of leading them in godliness.

How will you strategically make time to get to know your children so you can more effectively lead them in God's calling for their lives?

Conclusion

When God made Adam and Eve, it was his will for them to be fruitful and multiply (Gen 1:28). However, they were not just called to give birth to children, but to raise the children to be godly and to honor God with their lives (cf. Mal 2:15). And it's the same for us as parents.

How can we raise godly children?

1. In order to raise godly children, parents must model godliness.
2. In order to raise godly children, parents must train their children in God's Word.
3. In order to raise godly children, parents must discipline their children.
4. In order to raise godly children, parents must avoid provoking their children to anger.
5. In order to raise godly children, parents must know their children.

Raising Godly Children in Marriage Homework

Answer the questions, then discuss together.

1. What was new or stood out to you in this session? In what ways were you challenged or encouraged? Were there any points/thoughts that you did not agree with?

2. Would you agree that the most important aspect of raising godly children is the parents' consistency in modeling godliness? Why or why not? Are there areas in your life that you believe will not be a good model for your children? What about your mate? How can you address these areas to present a better model?

3. Moses commanded parents to impress the Word of God upon their own hearts and their children's (Deut 6:6-9). How are you currently trying to impress the Word of God on your heart? How will you impress the Word of God upon your children's hearts? What type of practices will you use?

4. How were you disciplined as a child (both punitive and non-punitive)? Do you think it was effective and how so? If not, why not?

5. What are your thoughts about Scripture's call for parents to use the "rod" to correct children (Prov 22:15)? What types of punitive disciplines do you plan on implementing with your children? How will you implement them?

6. What types of non-punitive disciplines do you plan on implementing with your children? Write down both the discipline and the desired character traits that should come from the discipline (i.e. by giving chores and allowance it will teach the child how to handle money, hard work, etc.). It may prove helpful to brainstorm.

7. Discuss this with your mate and come to some conclusions about types of discipline both non-punitive and punitive. Share conclusions and any anticipated areas of difficulty.

8. How have you seen or experienced children who have been provoked to wrath or rebellion by their parents? How will you protect your children from this?

9. How many children do you plan to have? How will you strategically take time to get to know each child individually?

10. After completing this session, how do you feel God is calling you to pray for your marriage? Spend some time praying.

Foundation Seven: Financial Faithfulness in Marriage

How can couples practice financial faithfulness in marriage? Many Christian couples give their tithe and offering to God but act like the rest is theirs. However, this is an incorrect use of finances. Psalm 24:1 says, "The earth is the LORD's, and everything in it, the world, and all who live in it." Crucial to financial faithfulness is recognizing that God is the owner, and we are simply stewards who will one day give an account (cf. Lk 19:15, Matt 25:19-20). When God created the earth, his intention was for humanity to rule over it under his dominion. To use his resources as though they were ours alone will always lead to unfaithfulness. Because of this predominant mindset among married couples, there is a constant misuse of finances, leading to financial stress.

Financial stress is one of the top reasons for marital conflict and divorce. This was never God's will. It was God's will for finances to be a source of blessing and a door for his overflowing grace in each marriage (cf. 1 Cor 9:6-11). But to be faithful and reap the blessings of God, couples must understand and follow God's plan for their finances.

How can couples practice financial faithfulness in marriage?

In Order to Be Financially Faithful, Couples Must Use Their Wealth to Win Souls for Christ

In Luke 16, Christ taught a parable to his disciples about wealth, to help them be faithful with it. We will consider this parable and apply it to married couples. This is what Christ said in Luke 16:1-13:

> "There was a rich man whose manager was accused of wasting his possessions. So he called him in and asked him, 'What is this I hear about you? Give an account of your management, because you cannot be manager any longer.' "The manager said to himself, 'What shall I do now? My master is taking away my job. I'm not strong enough to dig, and I'm ashamed to beg— I know what I'll do so that, when I lose my job here, people will welcome me into their houses.' "So he called in each one of his master's debtors. He asked the first, 'How much do you owe my master?' "'Eight hundred gallons of olive oil,' he replied. "The manager

83

told him, 'Take your bill, sit down quickly, and make it four hundred.' "Then he asked the second, 'And how much do you owe?' "'A thousand bushels of wheat,' he replied. "He told him, 'Take your bill and make it eight hundred.' "The master commended the dishonest manager because he had acted shrewdly. For the people of this world are more shrewd in dealing with their own kind than are the people of the light. I tell you, use worldly wealth to gain friends for yourselves, so that when it is gone, you will be welcomed into eternal dwellings. "Whoever can be trusted with very little can also be trusted with much, and whoever is dishonest with very little will also be dishonest with much. So if you have not been trustworthy in handling worldly wealth, who will trust you with true riches? And if you have not been trustworthy with someone else's property, who will give you property of your own? "No servant can serve two masters. Either he will hate the one and love the other, or he will be devoted to the one and despise the other. You cannot serve both God and Money."

Christ shared the story of an unjust steward who was misusing the master's money and, therefore, was going to be fired. Because of this, the steward devised a plan to provide for himself when he lost his job. The steward approached his master's debtors and gave them a discount, with the hope that they would provide for him when he lost his job. It almost appears as though Christ is praising this steward's dishonesty, but he is not. He praises his "shrewdness". This steward realized his future was uncertain and acted prudently to prepare for it.

Christ paralleled this with the Christian's preparation for eternity. Essentially, he said, in the same way the world seeks to provide for their earthly future (through storing up for retirement, making business connections, etc.), Christians must use worldly wealth to "gain friends" who will welcome them into "eternal dwellings" (v. 9).

What does he mean by eternal dwellings? Obviously, he was referring to heaven. Christ understood that to reach people with the gospel, money is needed. For churches to run and reach people in their neighborhood, it takes money. To send missionaries to other countries with the gospel, it costs money. Ministry work costs money. In fact, the Bible teaches those who "preach the gospel should get their living from the gospel" (1 Cor 9:14), meaning our teachers, pastors, and missionaries should be compensated for their work.

But not only was Christ stressing the need for Christians to give money to spread the gospel, he also was giving insight into a faithful steward's entrance into heaven. Christians who sacrificially give their money to advance the work of the gospel will be richly welcomed into heaven. People from other nations will surround them saying, "Through your support of this ministry, I accepted Christ and my family as well. Thank you." It seems that in heaven people will have a profound knowledge of what others did for the kingdom (cf. Matt 5:19, Rev 6:9). This shouldn't be a surprise, since those who do great things on earth are similarly honored. Days are named after them, streets, buildings, etc., and it seems to be similar in heaven. Those who generously give to advance the kingdom will be greatly welcomed and honored.

This should be the desire of every Christian couple. Christ commanded Christians to make friends in eternal dwellings by using their "worldly wealth" (v. 9). This is a calling that couples in developed nations can especially be fruitful in because of the amount of resources available to them.

With that said, Paul shared how the Macedonian churches, even though they were extremely poor, participated in this ministry as well. In 2 Corinthians 8:1-5, he said:

> And now, brothers, we want you to know about the grace that God has given the Macedonian churches. Out of the most severe trial, their overflowing joy and their extreme poverty welled up in rich generosity. For I testify that they gave as much as they were able, and even beyond their ability. Entirely on their own, they urgently pleaded with us for the privilege of sharing in this service to the saints. And they did not do as we expected, but they gave themselves first to the Lord and then to us in keeping with God's will.

Consider the Macedonian's wonderful testimony. In order to encourage the Corinthians to give, Paul told them about the Macedonian churches and their extreme generosity. He first clarifies their generosity came from a special work of God's grace (v. 1). God did a work within their hearts, which enabled them to give generously, even beyond their ability (v. 3). In fact, they pleaded with Paul for the privilege of helping struggling saints (v. 4). Isn't that amazing? They pleaded for the opportunity to give, even though they were poor themselves, and in this passage, they are forever memorialized for their sacrificial gifts.

That is what God desires for couples in marriage. He desires for them to sacrificially give to advance the kingdom. However, this is only possible if they, likewise, first give themselves to the Lord (v. 5). If couples hold back their lives, their passions, and their goals from God, then they will also hold back their wallets. When we give ourselves to the Lord, we will start to look more like him, being transformed from glory to glory (2 Cor 3:18). It was God who so loved the world that he gave his only begotten Son (John 3:16). This sacrificial lifestyle of giving should also be seen in his followers as they seek his approval in their stewardship.

The first principle couples must practice to be faithful with finances is to use their wealth to win souls for Christ and to build God's kingdom. Let us read our Lord's words again, "use worldly wealth to gain friends for yourselves, so that when it is gone, you will be welcomed into eternal dwellings" (v. 9).

In Order to Be Financially Faithful, Couples Must Focus on God's Reciprocal Blessings to Givers

After commanding his disciples to use their wealth to win souls, Christ gave them reasons why they should practice this. He says,

> "Whoever can be trusted with very little can also be trusted with much, and whoever is dishonest with very little will also be dishonest with much. So if you have not been trustworthy in handling worldly wealth, who will trust you with true riches? And if you have not been trustworthy with someone else's property, who will give you property of your own?
> Luke 16:10

He essentially said that if the disciples were faithful with their money, God would richly reward them with "true riches" on earth and in heaven, but if they were unfaithful, he couldn't trust them with more. We see this every day in our work world. A person starts working at a company with an entry level job. He works hard and is promoted by his manager. Good managers realize that those who are faithful with the small tasks will also be faithful with greater tasks. Therefore, they promote faithful workers and give them more responsibility. However, the unfaithful often lose responsibility and possibly their job. Similarly, God, our master, always watches how his children handle his money, and those who are faithful, he rewards with true riches.

What are the "true riches" God rewards his faithful stewards with? It probably refers, in part, to riches in heaven. In Matthew 6:19, Christ commanded Christians to store up riches in heaven that moth and rust cannot destroy. Similarly, in the Parable of the Minas, the faithful stewards received cities in the coming kingdom (Lk 19: 17, 19).

With that said, true riches refer to much more; it also refers to the discipleship of souls. Those who are faithful with money can be trusted with leading people, training them, caring for them, etc. This is part of the reason God requires elders to not love money and to run their own household well (1 Tim 3:3-4). Running one's household well includes faithfulness with finances. If a person is unfaithful with finances, he will be an unfaithful steward of people. However, when one is faithful with finances, God can entrust him with discipleship opportunities.

Furthermore, true riches probably refer to understanding and teaching the Word of God. Those who are faithful stewards of money will be faithful stewards of God's Word. And those who are not faithful will wrongly interpret and misuse Scripture.

Lastly, we gain more insight on "true riches" by considering Paul's teaching about God's promises to givers in 2 Corinthians 9:7-8. He says:

> Each man should give what he has decided in his heart to give, not reluctantly or under compulsion, for God loves a cheerful giver. And God is able to make all grace abound to you, so that in all things at all times, having all that you need, you will abound in every good work.

What other riches are bestowed upon those who faithfully give to populate the kingdom?

- God promises to love those are who are cheerful givers (v. 7). One might ask, "Doesn't God love everybody?" Certainly, but God only takes special pleasure in some (cf. James 2:23). He loves a cheerful giver—somebody who is happy to give. When we are liberal givers, we reflect God, which gives him great pleasure. This should be a motivation for couples.

God promises to give grace to meet all the needs of cheerful givers (v. 8). It says that God will make "all grace abound" so they have "all" they need. Many marriages struggle with lack simply because they are not faithful givers. In Malachi 2:8-9, God brings a curse on the Israelites as a consequence for robbing him in tithes and offerings. No doubt, many couples are similarly under a curse for robbing God.

- God promises to give grace to abound in "every good work" to cheerful givers. When he says there will be grace for "every good work," that includes much of what we have already considered. God will grace them with souls to shepherd and a growing understanding of Scripture. He will even give them grace to have a healthy marriage. Surely, marriage is a "good work" that God wants to lavishly pour his grace upon.

A couple who faithfully uses their little (money) to build God's kingdom will receive much (true riches). Through proper use of finances, a couple opens the door to an overflowing amount of grace given by God to and through their marriage. This principle is the door to great spiritual riches, great grace, and approval from God over a couple's stewardship.

In Order to Be Financially Faithful, Couples Must Not Love Money

To be faithful with finances, couples must also not love money. The desire for wealth and success can pull people away from God and, therefore, pull marriages apart. After teaching his disciples about how to use their money, Christ warned them by saying this:

> No servant can serve two masters. Either he will hate the one and love the other, or he will be devoted to the one and despise the other. You cannot serve both God and Money.
> Luke 16:13

Christ wanted the disciples to be aware of the danger of loving money. Similarly, Paul warned his disciple Timothy. He said:

> People who want to get rich fall into temptation and a trap and into many foolish and harmful desires that plunge men into ruin and destruction. For the love of money is a root of all kinds of evil. Some people, eager for money, have wandered from the faith and pierced themselves with many griefs.
> 1 Timothy 6:9-10

Paul warned Timothy of the consequences of loving money. Many plunged themselves into ruin and destruction because of it. Some even wandered from the faith and pierced themselves with countless griefs. Certainly, this has happened to many marriages as well.

In order to be faithful stewards of God's finances, couples must not love them. The apostle John said:

> Do not love the world or anything in the world. If anyone loves the world, the love of the Father is not in him. For everything in the world—the cravings of sinful man, the lust of his eyes and the boasting of what he has and does—comes not from the Father but from the world.
> 1 John 2:15-16

It is not that money or material possessions are necessarily bad in themselves. They are neutral; however, our hearts are bad. Our hearts are prone to ungodly cravings, lusts, and pride, which pull us away from God. And, when couples are pulled away from God, they will also be pulled away from one another.

It is good to think of marriage like a triangle. God is at the peak and the husband and wife are on opposite ends. The closer the husband and wife get towards God, the closer they will, by necessity, be with one another. But the farther they are away from God, the farther they will be from one another. Love for money and treasures have a tendency to pull couples away from God and from one another. Christ clearly said, "You cannot love both. You can only have one master."

Unfortunately, many couples fail to heed this warning, leading to rotten fruits in their marriage. In many homes, the husband works long hours to provide a better living for the family. However, work keeps him from spending quality time with his wife and children, and it also keeps him from being involved in church. Slowly, money becomes his god, and it destroys his relationship with his family. Many times the wife shares the same lust for more. In order to have more or to maintain what they have, both mates work long hours and the children are neglected, creating bitterness, resentment, and anger in their hearts. For this reason, we are raising a generation of rebellious children who are apathetic towards spiritual things and disrespectful towards authority. The god of money is destroying the home and, therefore, society.

Why is this so common among families? It's because riches have a tendency to deceive us. In the Parable of the Sower, Christ described the seed of the Word of God being sown into thorny ground. He said the worries of life and the "deceitfulness of wealth" choke the Word and make it unfruitful (Matt 13:22).

How do riches deceive people?

1. Riches deceive people into thinking only more will satisfy. How much is enough? The answer always is, "Just a little more." Therefore, people spend their lives trying to gain and find satisfaction in money and things, which only leave them unsatisfied.

2. Riches deceive people by blinding them (cf. Matt 6:21-23) and distorting their values. People start to put career and securing wealth above God, family, and people. This is because they have been blinded by their greed. Many times this leads them to do anything to gain wealth including breaking the law and hurting people.

3. Riches deceive people by promoting pride in those who possess it and insecurity in those who do not. The wealthy tend to exalt themselves and look disdainfully upon those who have less. In contrast, the poor often feel insecure and exalt the wealthy.

In order for couples to be faithful with their finances, they must not love money. Stress over money is one of the highest reasons for divorce because of its tendency to steal the hearts of one or both mates in marriage. Many in the church are really following money instead of God. Money dictates where to live, where to go to school, what job to take, where to go to church, who to marry or associate with, etc. We cannot serve two masters. The master, money, will destroy one's relationship with God and therefore one's marriage. The Master, God, will enhance and enrich both, if we allow him.

How can we tell if money is our master? We can tell by how we use our money. Christ said, "For where your treasure is, there your heart will be also" (Matt 6:21). Where people put their money shows where their heart is. Faithfully investing money into the kingdom demonstrates a heart for God. But those who primarily invest their money into the things of this world reveal a worldly heart. Therefore, we can tell who our master is by looking at our bank statements.

What does your use of money say about your heart and your relationship with God? Do you love God? Or do you love money and the things of this world? Loving money and the things of this world will grow weeds in your relationship with God and your marriage.

In Order to Be Financially Faithful, Couples Must Practice the Discipline of Simplicity

In addition to not loving money, couples must guard their hearts by practicing the discipline of simplicity. Because of our tendency to love treasures (cf. Matt 6:21), Christ commanded his followers to not store up riches on the earth. He said:

> Do not store up for yourselves treasures on earth, where moth and rust destroy, and where thieves break in and steal. But store up for yourselves treasures in heaven, where moth and rust do not destroy, and where thieves do not break in and steal."
> Matthew 6:19-20

To not store up treasures on earth is to practice the discipline of simplicity. How this is implemented will vary between each Christian. The disciples sold all in following Christ (cf. Lk 12:32), where others simply practiced moderation (cf. 1 Tim 6:17-19).

Now again, there is nothing intrinsically wrong with treasures, but there is something intrinsically wrong with our hearts. Therefore, Christ commanded Christians to not store up wealth, or anything that is a treasure, to protect our hearts.

What about saving? Does this mean that Christians should not save? Absolutely not. Scripture teaches us to save in order to meet our needs. Proverbs calls for us to consider the ant, how it stores up during the summer harvest for the winter (6:6-8). And so should Christians.

Then, what did Christ mean by the command to not store up treasures? What does it mean to practice the spiritual discipline of simplicity?

1. Simplicity means we should not trust in our wealth to provide for us (1 Tim 6:17). God is our provider. When Satan tempted Christ to turn stones into bread, he replied, "Man does not live by bread alone but by every word that comes from the mouth of God" (Matt 4:4). God is the one who commands the door to open for a job, a raise, a scholarship, housing, etc., in order to meet our daily needs. We must trust in him. Sadly, many couples are kept from doing God's will simply because their trust, really, is in their finances, their job, or their retirement.

2. Simplicity means we should practice moderation in our time devoted to the treasures of this world. Paul said that we should use the things of this world but not be "engrossed" in them (1 Cor 7:31). Video games, social media, Internet, and other creature-comforts have a tendency to consume people's hearts—creating distance in their relationship with God and their spouse. Moderation must be practiced.

3. Simplicity means we should practice moderation in our accumulation of wealth and the things of this world. We should consider this when

purchasing clothes, electronics, cars, furniture, homes, etc. James rebuked the early church for disobedience to Christ's command. He said the wealth they had stored up would testify against them in the last days. James 5:1-3 says this:

> Now listen, you rich people, weep and wail because of the misery that is coming upon you. Your wealth has rotted, and moths have eaten your clothes. Your gold and silver are corroded. Their corrosion will testify against you and eat your flesh like fire. You have hoarded wealth in the last days.

4. Simplicity means we must, at times, rid ourselves of certain treasures. With the rich man, his love for riches was keeping him from being saved (Matt 19:21-23). Wealth was his god. Therefore, he was commanded to leave his riches and follow Christ. Similarly, couples may have to make hard decisions about money, hobbies, career, etc., to really protect their relationship with God and one another.

What are your treasures? These have the potential of creating distance in relationships with God and your spouse. Many wives lament that their husbands spend so much time working, watching sports, spending time on the Internet, or playing video games. Many husbands feel like the home, shopping, beauty products, etc., get more attention from their wives than they do. Wealth and treasures have their proper place (cf. 1 Tim 6:17). Each couple must pray about and discern what the discipline of simplicity will look like in their marriage.

Some couples may feel called to sell all they have so they can focus on the kingdom, as the disciples did (Lk 12:32-33). Others may feel called to give up certain treasures (Matt 19:21) or to simply practice moderation with everything (1 Cor 7:31). We must be careful to not judge others for their convictions in this area (cf. Matt 7:1-2). Christ has called all his disciples to not store up (Matt 6:19). How has God called you to implement the discipline of simplicity to protect your hearts in marriage?

In Order to Be Financially Faithful, Couples Must Practice Living Debt-Free

The next principle couples must practice is staying debt-free. Romans 13:8 says, "Owe no man any thing, but to love one another: for he that loveth another hath fulfilled the law" (KJV). The NIV translates it, "Let no debt remain outstanding, except the continuing debt to love one another."

It is very interesting to consider the practical implications of this verse. Many people want to love others through giving liberally and serving radically but feel like they can't because of debt. They have a house payment, car payments, college payments, credit card payments, etc., which keep them from paying their "continuing debt of loving one another."

In order to liberally give and radically serve, couples must pay their debts and practice staying out of debt. This may call for significant life changes. For those still going to college or graduate school, this could mean going to a less expensive, and possibly less reputable, university to lower debt. It could mean being resourceful by finding ways to lower college debt through obtaining scholarships, working while in school, lengthening the time it takes to finish, living inexpensively, etc.

For others, staying out of debt could mean buying a used car and avoiding car payments. I heard a famous TV show host say one time, "I never purchase a new car! It drops thousands of dollars right after leaving the lot. I let somebody else buy it new, and then I buy it cheaper with low mileage."

For others, it could mean renting instead of buying a home or not buying their "dream home". It should be noted that though the norm in today's society is to own a home, it might not be God's will for you. Abraham never owned a home; he lived in tents though he was a rich man (Hebrews 11:9). It was also normal in Abraham's time to own, but he chose not to because he saw himself as a pilgrim waiting for his heavenly home. Hebrews 11:9-10 says this about him:

> By faith he made his home in the promised land like a stranger in a foreign country; he lived in tents, as did Isaac and Jacob, who were heirs with him of the same promise. For he was looking forward to the city with foundations, whose architect and builder is God.

Christ also did not own a home. It probably would have hindered his ability to minister. He once declared, "Foxes have holes and birds of the air have nests, but the Son of Man has no place to lay his head" (Luke 9:58). It has been a common practice throughout the centuries for ministers to not own to be more available for God's purposes.

Whenever a person is in debt, he is a slave to the lender (Prov 22:7), which comes with restrictions. However, Scripture commands us to only be slaves of God (cf. Matt 6:24) and to avoid being slaves of others (1 Cor 7:23). Debt will often deter your allegiance from God and keep you from paying your continuing debt of loving others (Rom 13:8).

How is God calling you to practice staying debt free?

In Order to Be Financially Faithful, Couples Must Practice Increasing Their Giving to God's Work

The last principle couples must practice to be faithful with their finances is continually seeking to increase giving. Typically, when Christians get more money, they respond just like the world. They put their money into a bigger house, nicer car, new clothes, the newest phone and electronic gadgets, etc. However, Scripture teaches God blesses us so we can bless others (cf. 2 Cor 8:14-15, Gen 12:2) and that we should continually increase our giving. Listen to what Paul told the Corinthians about giving:

> Now concerning the collection for the saints, as I have given order to the churches of Galatia, even so do ye. Upon the first day of the week let every one of you lay by him in store, as God hath prospered him, that there be no gatherings when I come.
> 1 Corinthians 16:1-2 KJV

Paul told the Corinthians to give as God "prospered" them or it can also be translated "in keeping with your income." When God prospers a couple, they should increase their giving. In fact, Paul taught this same principle in 2 Corinthians 8:7, "But just as you excel in everything—in faith, in speech, in knowledge, in complete earnestness and in your love for us—see that you also *excel in this grace of giving.*" He said in the same way Christians continually seek to excel in godly virtues, they should continually seek to excel in the grace of giving.

When a couple gets married, it should be their goal to grow in their giving every year, if the Lord wills. They should periodically look at their finances and discern if the Lord is calling them to increase their offerings. With that said, unplanned events or a decrease in income may require a decrease in giving. But, in general, God's desire is for couples to grow in giving.

Are you desiring and trying to consistently grow in your giving? What changes need to be made to give more?

Conclusion

God, our master, is returning, and when he does, there will be an accounting of our financial faithfulness. Have you been faithful stewards of the Lord's money? If couples are going to be financially faithful, they must understand and follow God's plan for their finances.

1. In order to be financially faithful, couples must use their wealth to win souls for Christ.
2. In order to be financially faithful, couples must focus on God's reciprocal blessing to givers.
3. In order to be financially faithful, couples must not love money.
4. In order to be financially faithful, couples must practice the discipline of simplicity.
5. In order to be financially faithful, couples must practice living debt-free.
6. In order to be financially faithful, couples must practice increasing their giving to God's work.

Financial Faithfulness in Marriage Homework

Answer the questions, then discuss together.

1. What was new or stood out to you in this session? In what ways were you challenged or encouraged? Were there any points/thoughts that you did not agree with?

2. Typically, in each marriage, there is a saver and a spender. Discerning this and talking about it beforehand may help protect your marriage from some bumps and bruises down the road.

    How do you typically use your money? What do you spend it on? What percentage do you save? What percentage do you give to the Lord's work? What about your mate?

3. Who would you consider the spender and the saver in the relationship? Do you have any concerns about your spending or saving habits? How could you improve your spending and saving?

4. Do you have any concerns about your spouse's spending or saving habits? In what ways could your spouse improve his or her spending and saving?

5. What would you consider "treasures" that potentially could steal your heart away from God and your spouse? This could be anything that consumes your thoughts and time such as: relationships, Internet, school, clothes, movies, music, video games, money, work, success, etc. How do you feel God is calling you to be more disciplined in these areas? What about your mate?

6. Imagine that you were approached to help persecuted Christians in North Korea. Christians there are being raped, killed, and imprisoned every day. Finances are needed to support underground missionaries to teach the Word, bring Bibles in the country, and to minister to the persecuted and oppressed. You have committed to helping this cause for the next five years in conjunction with faithfully giving to your church. What lifestyle changes can you make now to live more simply to give more? How can

you and your mate be more economical? Consider that both of you are working unless you know one partner will not be.

7. Consider the possibility that you and your spouse will have a baby within two years and you will have to live on one income. Could you live on one income? What could you do to cut down expenses in order to promote greater savings? Are you willing to live in an apartment instead of a house? Are there any long-standing debts that it might be prudent to pay off now? Are there trainings, schooling or other preparations that you should complete to be more economically stable in the future?

Consider that it is always good as a lifetime practice to budget as though you only had one income, not only for pregnancy, but sickness, loss of job, unforeseen problems, etc. Write down a plan to *prepare to live on one income throughout marriage.*

8. Consider the possibility of being a couple that always wants to increase their financial giving to kingdom work. A wise practice to consider with your giving is to begin by giving a tithe, and as God prospers you, increase it (cf. 1 Cor. 16:2, 2 Cor 8:7). Pray and ask God what percentage to start with in your giving and what percentage you want to reach by living simply over the next five years?

9. Proverbs 27:23-24 says, "Be sure you know the condition of your flocks, give careful attention to your herds; for riches do not endure forever, and a crown is not secure for all generations." It is a good practice to always budget so you know the amount of money you have, where it is going, and your short-term and long-term goals for it. If you don't always know the condition of your flocks, a great loss could cause unexpected stress on your family.

Make a sample budget taking into consideration that you are married and living either in an apartment or a house. Include such things as: tithe and offerings, savings, cell phone, rent or mortgage, gas, food, insurance, fun, etc.

10. How much will it cost to live comfortably, save, and generously give to the Lord? Are there any concerns and/or adjustments that might need to be made?

11. After completing this session, how do you feel God is calling you to pray for your marriage? Spend some time praying.

98

Foundation Eight: Intimacy in Marriage

How should couples develop intimacy in marriage?

Marriage should be the most intimate relationship anybody experiences in life. It should be more intimate than a friendship, a mother-daughter relationship, a father-son relationship, a boyfriend-girlfriend relationship, etc. But sadly, many couples often feel distant and alone in marriage.

Because man is body, soul, and spirit (cf. 1 Thess 5:23, Heb 4:12), married couples must cultivate each aspect of their being in order to develop intimacy. They must cultivate their friendship (soul), their sexuality (body), and their spirituality (spirit) in marriage. If one aspect of this tri-unity is missing, couples will lack the intimacy God desires. Therefore, all three must be continually cultivated.

How should married couples develop these three aspects of intimacy?

Intimacy in Friendship

As we consider developing intimacy in friendship, we must consider Christ and his friendship with the church. Jesus said this in John 15:15:

> I no longer call you servants, because a servant does not know his master's business. Instead, I have called you friends, for everything that I learned from my Father I have made known to you.

What makes the difference between being Christ's servant and his friend? It was the fact that Christ shared everything with his friends. As the church, we are both Christ's bride (cf. Eph 5:23-27) and his friend. He has taught us his secrets, things that the world will not and cannot understand (1 Cor 2:14). Through his Word and the Holy Spirit, he has taught us truths about salvation, mankind, creation, angels and demons, and the future. As the church, we are Christ's friends, and every day we have the privilege to grow in intimacy with him through studying his Word and speaking with him in prayer.

Similarly, this practice of communing through sharing one's life, thoughts, fears, and concerns will cultivate a married couple's friendship and therefore intimacy. Certainly, there is a need for discipline in this area. As life gets busy with work, managing the household, raising children, church, hobbies, etc., there will be many things (some good things) that can distract from cultivating the friendship.

99

Likewise, this often happens in our relationship with God. Remember the story of Mary and Martha? Martha was busy serving, while Mary quietly sat at Jesus' feet. In the same way, we often get busy with good things, which can cause us to neglect our relationship with God. This can also happen with our spouse, causing not only a lack of intimacy but discord in marriage.

What disciplines can couples practice to cultivate their friendship?

1. Couples should practice setting aside a period of time every day for sharing and listening to cultivate their friendship.

Activities are good, but intimate sharing should be maximized when couples are together. For most, evenings will be the best time for this, after work and other endeavors are completed.

Personally, my wife and I always try to leave the last hour or more of the evening for sharing and prayer. We may have family time before that where we eat dinner, talk, watch a TV show together with our daughter, etc., but with the last part of the evening, we want to focus on one another.

As a couple has more children, it becomes even harder to allot time for intimate sharing, but it is still just as important. I heard one pastor's wife, who had five children, share that in their home, the children had to be in their rooms by eight pm. She would commonly tell their kids after eight pm, "I am no longer Mom but my husband's wife." That's how they managed a busy home and yet kept intimacy. It also demonstrated to the kids the priority of the marriage relationship.

2. Couples should be careful of *intimacy killers* to focus on cultivating their friendship.

In considering the importance of time alone, one should be aware of intimacy killers. Though I mentioned watching TV with my wife, I am aware that this does not create genuine intimacy, but commonly distracts from it. Often watching TV, being on the Internet, playing video games, being on the phone, etc., can be ways of distracting from or avoiding intimacy.

One marital counseling book my wife and I read early on in marriage encouraged couples to not turn on the TV for the first year of marriage. The first year of marriage is foundational for the rest of marriage. In the Old Testament, a soldier was not allowed to go to war during the first year of marriage. He was to stay home and bring his wife happiness (Deut 24:5). It is within the first year of marriage that patterns are established, both healthy and unhealthy ones. If a couple establishes early patterns of primarily *watching and doing* instead of *being and sharing*, it may reap hazardous dividends later in marriage. It is not uncommon for couples to say after years of marriage, "We realized that we really didn't know one another." It is very possible these couples established unhealthy patterns early in marriage of being distracted by intimacy killers, which kept them from ever truly knowing one another.

This is good to consider about marriage and especially one's first year, which establishes a foundation for the rest of marriage. Do you want to have a marriage where your mate comes home, kisses you on the cheek, and then gets on the Internet, TV, or phone for three hours before bed? It is good to beware of these tendencies which can potentially hurt couples. Protect yourself from intimacy killers; block out daily time to focus on sharing, listening, and being together.

3. Couples should enjoy activities together to cultivate their friendship.

With all that said, balance is needed in marriage. Couples need times of just sharing and listening to one another, but they also need to enjoy activities together such as: reading, working out, going to movies, traveling, etc. Sadly, many couples get married believing they have many activities they love doing together, but after the first year, they find that they really enjoy different things. While courting, the woman would watch sports with her boyfriend because she was just happy to be with him. However, soon after getting married, she would quickly decline watching the Sunday football game to do her own thing. While courting, the man would go to the mall with his girlfriend because he was just happy to be around her. However, in marriage, he promptly declines the Saturday excursion to instead stay home. It is not uncommon for early passion to blur the reality of the person one is going to marry, and couples should be aware of this.

Whether this happens or not, it is important for couples to find activities they enjoy together, to help maintain and increase intimacy. Christ went everywhere with his infant church, the disciples, and shared everything with them (cf. Matt 17:1, John 15:15). To protect our marriages and help them grow, it is wise to think about and plan for activities that can be enjoyed together as well as setting weekly or monthly dates to share these things. "The plans of the diligent lead to profit as surely as haste leads to poverty" (Proverbs 21:5).

Of course, many times husbands and wives will simply not enjoy the same activities. This is normal. However, out of love for their spouse, they should participate in many of the activities their spouse enjoys. The wife should occasionally watch the football game, and the husband should occasionally watch the romantic comedy. Out of love, we should serve our mate, and one of the greatest ways to do this is by doing something he or she enjoys. This will enrich the friendship.

4. Couples should establish a weekly date night to cultivate their friendship.

In addition, a wise practice for couples is to establish a weekly date night. Choose a convenient night of the week to go out and do something special. Guard this night from the rigors of busyness, and when unforeseen circumstances do not allow it, always reschedule. Date night does not have to be expensive or even cost money; the most important aspect of it is spending uninterrupted time together.

One of the great realities of marriage is that it will take a lifetime to truly know your spouse since he or she is always growing and changing. Therefore, as a discipline, wisely plan to cultivate the intimacy of friendship in marriage.

Intimacy in Sex

Next, couples must cultivate intimacy through sex. God meant sex to be a powerful means of increasing intimacy in marriage. In fact, it has often been called the "litmus test" of marriage. Couples who are angry with one another will eat together, go to the movies together, and church together but most likely will not have sex together. Sex is a gauge for a couple's intimacy and, also, how a couple increases it.

If a married couple finds themselves going weeks without sex, it may be a good time to evaluate the relationship. "Are my spouse and I alright?" "Am I meeting his/her needs?"

In considering sex, it is also important to consider Satan's tactics in that area of marriage. While unmarried, his energy focuses on tempting couples towards premarital sex, but in marriage, his energy focuses on tempting them to not have sex. Young married couples will often find this a paradox since their passion was hard to contain before marriage. But in the marriage union, sexual intimacy tends to become dry and stagnant. Satan wants to hinder a married couple's intimacy through a lack of sex. We will consider Satan's work more later in this session.

For now, let's consider God's purposes for sex.

1. God's purpose for sex is as a means of *unity and intimacy* in marriage.

Genesis 2:24 says: "For this reason a man will leave his father and mother and be united to his wife, and they will become one flesh." When the narrator said the man and woman become "one flesh," he was referring directly to sex. This is supported by the fact that 1 Corinthian 6:16 says a man who has sex with a harlot becomes "one flesh" with her. The sexual act was meant to be a symbol of unity and intimacy in marriage and how a couple cultivated them.

In fact, sex was used to picture God's intimacy and covenant with the nation of Israel. Ezekiel 16:8 says:

> Later I passed by, and when I looked at you and saw that you were old enough for love, I spread the corner of my garment over you and covered your nakedness. I gave you my solemn oath and entered into a covenant with you, declares the Sovereign LORD, and you became mine.

God took Israel as his wife, as a husband took his virgin wife to himself. God meant sex in marriage to symbolize the most intimate relationship in the world, our relationship with him. It is a powerful union. It is both a symbol of unity and intimacy and the means of how a married couple grows in them.

2.   God's purpose for sex is as a means of *procreation*.

As mentioned in session one, God desires for couples to birth and raise godly seed. Consider these verses:

> So God created man in his own image, in the image of God he created him; male and female he created them. God blessed them and said to them, 'Be fruitful and increase in number; fill the earth and subdue it. Rule over the fish of the sea and the birds of the air and over every living creature that moves on the ground.
> Genesis 1:27-38

> Has not the LORD made them one? In flesh and spirit they are his. And why one? Because he was seeking godly offspring. So guard yourself in your spirit, and do not break faith with the wife of your youth.
> Malachi 2:15

3.   God's purpose for sex is as a means of enjoyment and pleasure.

Consider these verses:

> May your fountain be blessed, and may you rejoice in the wife of your youth. A loving doe, a graceful deer— may her breasts satisfy you always, may you ever be captivated by her love.
> Proverbs 5:18-19

> How beautiful you are and how pleasing, O love, with your delights! Your stature is like that of the palm, and your breasts like clusters of fruit. I said, "I will climb the palm tree; I will take hold of its fruit." May your breasts be like the clusters of the vine, the fragrance of your breath like apples, and your mouth like the best wine. May the wine go straight to my lover, flowing gently over lips and teeth. I belong to my lover, and his desire is for me. Come, my lover, let us go to the countryside, let us spend the night in the villages. Let us go early to the vineyards to see if the vines have budded, if their blossoms have opened, and if the pomegranates are in bloom—there I will give you my love.
> Song of Songs 7:6-12

Couples are meant to enjoy their spouse through sex. In a very real way, sex is a celebration of the relationship, a way to express pleasure in one another.

4. God's purpose in sex is as a means of serving one's spouse.

In 1 Corinthians 7:3-4, Paul said:

> The husband should fulfill his marital duty to his wife, and likewise the wife to her husband. The wife's body does not belong to her alone but also to her husband. In the same way, the husband's body does not belong to him alone but also to his wife. Do not deprive each other except by mutual consent and for a time, so that you may devote yourselves to prayer. Then come together again so that Satan will not tempt you because of your lack of self-control.

Paul taught the wife must give her husband the right of ownership of her body, and the husband must do the same (v. 4). They should not withhold sex as a weapon to get their way or to punish their mate. Paul explicitly said to not "deprive each other" except temporarily by "mutual consent" for spiritual reasons (v. 5).

When I got married, I received counsel about sex from a godly man. He said when he first got married, he and his wife made an agreement. When angry or when one didn't desire to have sex, one would still offer oneself to the other as Scripture teaches. He or she would say to the other, *"I may not feel like it now, but if you will take me like this, I want to serve you."* Married couples must learn to view sex as a ministry to one another and commit to always be available to fulfill their mate's need.

Sadly, sex in marriage is often about fulfilling one's lust or reaching one's own climax instead of serving. Consequently, a spouse can still feel used and/or unsatisfied sexually in marriage. However, this was never God's plan. Philippians 2:3-4 says this:

> Do nothing out of selfish ambition or vain conceit, but in humility consider others better than yourselves. Each of you should look not only to your own interests, but also to the interests of others.

In sex, as with every relationship, nothing should be done out of selfish motivation but primarily to serve the interests of the other. In sex, the husband's goal should be his wife's pleasure, and the wife's goal should be her husband's pleasure.

How does this work when spouses have different libidos? In most marriages, one spouse desires sex more than the other. Because God's plan for sex in marriage is for each spouse to seek the pleasure of the other, this means that one spouse will have sex more than desired, and the other will have less than desired. Each should continually seek to serve the interest of the other within the sexual relationship.

Obviously, no one should feel forced, but if a spouse is lacking desire to serve his/her mate, the spouse should pray and ask God for grace to serve. In fact, it is a wise practice for mates to continually pray to serve their mate better in the sexual union. By serving their mate, they are honoring God and his design for marriage.

Moreover, couples should minister to one another sexually with the understanding that there is grace available (cf. James 4:6, Gal 5:22-23, John 15:5). God desires to give couples grace to love, to serve, and to bless their sexual union because this is his will for marriage. Each couple should regularly petition God for his anointing over their union.

5. God's purpose for sex is as a means of protection from sexual immorality and other temptations.

First Corinthians 7:1-2 says, "Now for the matters you wrote about: It is good for a man not to marry. But since there is so much immorality, each man should have his own wife, and each woman her own husband."

Paul taught that marriage, and sex in marriage, was meant to protect couples from temptations towards sexual immorality. In fact, Paul added this:

> Do not deprive each other except by mutual consent and for a time, so that you may devote yourselves to prayer. Then come together again so that Satan will not tempt you because of your lack of self-control.
> 1 Corinthians 7:5

When couples do not practice consistency in sex, it allows Satan to tempt them in various ways. In what ways does Satan tempt couples for lack of sexual consistency?

Of course, he tempts them sexually through lust, pornography, adultery, etc. But there are many other temptations, such as one or both mates feeling unloved, undesired, depressed, and/or insecure. I have found this very common for wives, especially after having children. When the sexual union is not consistent, they are tempted to feel unattractive and unloved. It becomes an open door for Satan to trample the woman in marriage. With the husband, when the sexual union is inconsistent, it seems he is more prone to be tempted sexually. This might be because the husband more commonly works outside the home around members of the opposite sex. It is wise for husbands and wives to view their sexual intimacy as a necessary protection from the evil one's schemes.

As an example, I had one friend share that when he first got married, Satan focused his attacks on the bedroom. It became a tremendous source of insecurity, fears, and discord. Many couples would say the same thing. For this reason couples must practice faithfulness in this area and view it, not only as a way to enhance their marriage, but to guard their marriage. Some churches in recent years have developed marriage campaigns where couples commit to having sex every day for a week or a month as a spiritual discipline to increase the health of marriages. This may be over the top, but the principle behind it is very biblical.

Personally, I think it is wise for couples to establish a weekly plan to practice sexual intimacy. Satan will use busyness, tiredness, children, ministry, etc., to keep couples from the blessing of sex. Proverbs 21:5 says, "The plans of the diligent lead to profit as surely as haste leads to poverty." Those who plan, plan to succeed, and those who do not plan, plan to fail.

Let me add a caution about when couples have children. The birth of children adds new challenges to a couple's intimacy. The children stage is a tremendous blessing, but it will open more doors for Satan to attack sexual intimacy in marriage. Many times children become the focus of the marriage. In some cultures, the wife will often co-sleep with the child for years. In those scenarios, couples will have to be even more strategic. Satan is not going to stop attacking the marriage because of children. In fact, his attacks will probably increase. Therefore, Christians must be wise and strategic in how they protect the sexual union.

With all that said, what are some ways to enrich sex in marriage?

- openly talk about it
- set up dates for it
- practice flirting throughout the day
- pray about it
- be creative
- wisely read Christian literature about it

Christian literature can offer insights without being tasteless and irreverent. For instance, God made the woman's body differently than the man's. The woman's body typically takes longer to arouse, and they are stirred more emotionally than men. In order for the husband to serve the woman, it will typically start long before entering the bedroom through touch, communication, and loving service.

In summary, sex is a celebration that God created to enrich marriage. It is where intimacy and unity are cultivated, where the miracle of procreation happens, and where pure joy is stimulated. However, it is also an area where Satan commonly attacks. Couples must guard it and cultivate it to grow in intimacy with one another.

Intimacy in the Spiritual

The final way of building intimacy is through cultivating spiritual intimacy. This may be the most neglected aspect of intimacy in marriages. People cultivate the mind and the body but often forget the spirit. Many couples in marriage, even marriages lasting over twenty years, commonly say to themselves, "There is something missing." The spiritual aspect is often the missing link to a successful marriage.

One of the aspects that distinguish man and animal is the fact that God gave man a spirit to commune with him. It is the highest function of humanity, and when it is neglected, man, in one sense, resembles animals. They are driven simply by their basic instincts to feed, to have sex, to have security, and to have power. Mankind was meant to have a relationship with God. In the Genesis narrative, it continually shows how man walked and talked with God (cf. Gen 2:16-17, 5:24, 6:9, 13). When couples cultivate their spiritual life together, they greatly increase intimacy with one another.

What are some ways for couples to increase spiritual intimacy?

1. Couples should schedule times of seeking God through prayer and God's Word as a family (cf. 1 Cor 7:5).

This could be done every night and/or morning, once or twice a week, or even at meal times. In general, couples should try to incorporate prayer and Scripture as much as possible, when starting the day, when driving, when eating, before going to church, before putting the children to sleep, etc. (cf. Deut 6:6-9).

2. Couples should worship with other Christians weekly.

This should be done by becoming a member of a Bible preaching church and participating in Sunday service, small groups, prayer meetings, etc. The Bible commands us to "not neglect" the gathering of one another together for the purpose of encouragement (Hebrews 10:25). With this, married couples will generally find it very enriching to develop spiritual connections with other Christian couples in the same stage of life and also with those who can help mentor them.

3. Couples should find ways of serving God and others together.

Hospitality should definitely be one avenue of serving. Hebrews 13:1-2 says: "Keep on loving each other as brothers. Do not forget to entertain strangers, for by so doing some people have entertained angels without knowing it." Couples should open their home to bless others. However, serving should not be limited to hospitality. God may call some couples to invest in ministry to teenagers, children, neighbors, the homeless, widows, etc.

How will you cultivate your spiritual life together in marriage? Certainly, couples should not neglect their own individual devotions, worship, and gifts, but in becoming "one flesh" in marriage (Gen 2:24), they should also cultivate their spiritual life together.

Conclusion

Intimacy is a very important part of marriage. God made man a tri-unity with a body, soul, and spirit (cf. 1 Thess 5:23, Heb 4:12), and each of these must be cultivated to develop intimacy in marriage. Couples do this by cultivating their friendship (soul), their sexuality (body), and their spirituality (spirit). Developing a plan to cultivate these three aspects of intimacy will greatly enrich one's marriage.

How is God calling you to strategically develop intimacy in marriage?

Intimacy in Marriage Homework

Answer the questions, then discuss together.

1. What was new or stood out to you in this session? In what ways were you challenged or encouraged? Were there any points/thoughts that you did not agree with?

2. How would you describe intimacy and the importance of it in marriage?

3. Are there any known variables that you think could possibly detract from daily time alone with your spouse and intimate sharing (i.e. work, hobbies, personality, fear, etc.)? What intimacy killers do you and your mate have to be careful of? How will you navigate these to cultivate your friendship?

4. Write down seven activities you enjoy doing for fun. Write down seven activities your spouse enjoys doing for fun. What activities will you and your spouse do together? What activities are you willing to learn how to do or enjoy to further cultivate your friendship?

5. How will you cultivate a healthy sexual relationship to protect your marriage from the evil one's temptations (cf. 1 Cor 7:5)? How will you keep your sex life from stagnation?

6. What will you do in marriage when you and/or your mate start to lose love for one another? Revelation 2:4-5 offers principles that can help protect and restore love in marriage. It says:

> Yet I hold this against you: You have forsaken your first love. Remember the height from which you have fallen! Repent and do the things you did at first. If you do not repent, I will come to you and remove your lamp stand from its place.

The context of this verse is Jesus speaking to the church of Ephesus who had lost passion for him. The church was excelling in many things (v. 1-3): preaching, teaching, hating false doctrine, and righteousness, but they had lost the most important thing—their first love for Christ.

Love is the most important part of our relationship with God. That is why the greatest commandment is to love God with our whole heart, mind, and soul (Matt 22:36-37). Because the church of Ephesus had lost this, Christ promised to discipline them by taking away their lampstand—their light in the community, which would ultimately destroy the church.

Similarly, love is the most important part of marriage. Therefore, the counsel Christ gave this church can be applied to restoring love in marriage. Christ called for this church to restore their love by repenting (recognizing and turning away from sin) and doing what they did when they first started to love God (maybe extensive time in the Word and prayer, church fellowship, service, etc.). This type of response to a lack of love is also needed in marriage to maintain or restore intimacy.

What type of things did you originally do when you fell in love with your spouse? How can you continually cultivate these to keep your first love or restore it?

7. After completing this session, how do you feel God is calling you to pray for your marriage? Spend some time praying.

Closing Thoughts

Congratulations on finishing the *Building Foundations for a Godly Marriage* curriculum! I would like to leave you with a few closing thoughts. In Deuteronomy 24:5, God called for soldiers to not go to war during their first year of marriage. He said:

If a man has recently married, he must not be sent to war or have any other duty laid on him. For one year he is to be free to stay at home and bring happiness to the wife he has married.

In this, a clear principle is established showing how important the first year of marriage is. Statistics support this; one of the highest years of divorce is the first year. Everything will be new, and in this year, you will build habits that will sustain or hurt you for the rest of your marriage. Therefore, it is important to be very intentional within your first year.

As shared earlier in the book, one marriage guru said that couples should not watch any TV within the first year of marriage to focus on one another. Though this may be an overstatement, the basic principle behind this statement is true. Couples need to develop a pattern of focus within the first year that will continue throughout the marriage.

For example, in my first year of marriage, my wife and I decided that she would not work full-time and I stopped pursuing further education, so we could focus on one another. Plus, we had a brief courtship, so getting to know one another was even more important for us.

Couples should be very careful about taking on extra tasks in the first year that will keep them away from one another. They should spend as much quality time together as possible, building a foundation for a long and healthy marriage.

Another principle that I will leave you with is the importance of having a mentor or a mentor couple. Think of a strong Christian married couple who would serve as good mentors. You could meet together once a month, pray together, do a Bible study together, or simply secure the right to call them for godly advice and invite them to check in on you throughout the marriage.

There is support for this in Paul's call for older women to mentor younger women. In Titus 2:3-5, Paul says this:

Likewise, teach the older women to be reverent in the way they live, not to be slanderers or addicted to much wine, but to teach what is good. Then they can train the younger women to love their husbands and children, to be self-controlled and pure, to be busy at home, to be kind, and to be subject to their husbands, so that no one will malign the word of God.

For a new job, we go through training. How much more do we need continual training in marriage? You will find mentorship invaluable for your future, and one day you will pass on the wisdom you gained to another couple. May God richly bless and strengthen your marriage.

Bibliography

Barclay, William. *The New Daily Study Bible: The Letters to
    Philippians, Colossians, and Thessalonians*, 3rd ed. (Louisville, KY;
    London: Westminster John Knox Press, 2003), 190.

"Discipline", accessed 2/7/15
    http://dictionary.reference.com/browse/discipline.

Hawkins, Ronald E. *Strengthening Marital Intimacy.* USA: Baker
    Book House Company, 1991.

Keathley, J. III. *The Principle of Nature (Knowing Your Child),*
    accessed 2/8/15 https://bible.org/seriespage/principle-nature-knowing-
    your-child .

Miller, Kathy Collars, D. Larry Miller and Larry Richards. *What's
    in the Bible for Couples.* Minnesota: Bethany House, 2007.

Parrot, Les and Leslie. *Saving Your Marriage Before It Starts.*
    Grand Rapids, MI: Zondervan, 2006.

Rainey, Dennis. *Preparing for Marriage.* California: Gospel Light,
    1997.

Wes, Roberts and H. Norman Wright. *Before You Say "I Do".*
    Oregon: Harvest House Publishers, 1997.

Worthington, Everett L. *Hope-Focused Marriage Counseling: A
    Guide to Brief Therapy.* Downers Grove: Intervarsity Press,
    1999.

Sample Counseling First Session

Pre-session:

If the counselor prefers, the couple will fill out the relationship questionnaire before the first session (see Appendix 2).

Counselor Introduction:

The counselor will share a brief testimony, including his background, his own marriage (if married), his counseling experience, and his hope for this session. Then, the counselor will ask the couple questions to get to know them better.

Questions for the Couple:

(Or, instead of asking questions in the session, the counselor can simply follow up on questions from the relationship questionnaire.)

Please share your individual backgrounds: where you are from, your family background, your education background, and anything else you would like to share.

Please share how you and your fiancé(e) met, how long you've known each other, and how you knew you were meant to be together.

Please share your religious experience. Are you a born again believer? Do you have assurance of salvation? What is your involvement in church?

Please share ways you and your fiancé(e) are similar. Share ways you are different. How can these similarities and differences complement your marriage?

How do you get along with your parents? What was their parenting style like? What did you like and dislike about it? What will you take from your parents and add to your marriage?

What are your hopes for going through pre-marital counseling?

Course Overview:

Counselor will share the course overview and expectations. For example:

This pre-marital course will cover eight different foundations of marriage including: God's plan for marriage, gender roles, finances, communication, raising godly children, etc.

Each week you will:

1. *Read the lesson and complete the homework individually. It should take around one to two hours to complete.*

2. *Discuss the answers to your homework with your mate. After your discussion, you should spend time praying together about your future marriage. Also, think about any questions you might have for me (the counselor). Send me your answers and questions before our session together.*

3. *Meet with me to discuss your answers and questions. I will share any additional insights and pray with you. This should take no more than an hour. (Or the counselor can respond through email and only meet sparingly if preferred).*

Closing:

Any questions? Session 1 "God's Plan for Marriage" will be your first assignment. Let's meet next week at this same time. Let's close in prayer.

Relational History Questionnaire

Please respond to the following questions so I can prepare an assessment after our first meeting. We will discuss some of these questions while getting to know one another.

1. Define marriage. What is its purpose?

2. List ways you and your fiancé(e) are similar? List ways you are different?

3. How can these similarities and differences complement your marriage?

4. Describe your relationship, as a child, with your parents? What were they like? What did you like and dislike about their methods? Are there any things you would like to model or not model in your marriage?

5. What was your spiritual life like as a child? How has it changed since then?

6. What is your previous relationship history? How does it affect you in your present relationship?

7. What do you enjoy reading and watching on TV?

8. Have you ever had a child? Do you want children in the future? If so, how many do you want?

9. What was your family's financial situation as a youth?

10. Describe briefly your education and job experience.

11. Describe a routine work day starting from when you wake up till you go to sleep?

12. What do you do for fun?

13. Describe some things you and your fiancé(e) usually disagree over or fight over? What does a fight look like?

14. Please share how you and your fiancé(e) met and how you were led to commit to one another in marriage.

15. Share your religious experience. Are you a born again believer? What is your involvement in church?

16. When do you plan on getting married? What type of wedding do you plan on having?

Get To Know One Another

Consider investing in your future marriage by taking tests that will help you know one another more, understand one another, and better serve one another. Your marriage is worth the investment.

1.   Take the Myer Briggs Personality Test and discuss with one another.

http://www.mbtionline.com/TakeTheAssessment

What did you learn about yourself and your mate, and how can it be helpful in marriage?

2.   Take the Five Love Languages Test and discuss with one another.

http://www.5lovelanguages.com/

What did you learn about yourself and your mate, and how can it be helpful in marriage?

3.   Take the Strengthfinders 2.0 test and discuss with one another.

http://www.strengthstest.com/strengths-tests/strengthsfinder-20-access-code.html

What did you learn about yourself and your mate, and how can it be helpful in marriage?

Study Group Tips

Leading a small group using the *Bible Teacher's Guide* can be done in various ways. One format for leading a small group is the "study group" model, where each member prepares and shares in the teaching. This appendix will cover tips for facilitating a weekly study group.

1. Each week the members of the study group will read through a select chapter of the guide, complete the homework, answer the *reflection questions* (see Appendix 5), and come prepared to share in the group.

2. Prior to each meeting, a different member can be selected to lead the group and share Question 1 of the reflection questions, which is to give a short summary of the chapter read. This section of the gathering could last from five to fifteen minutes. This way, each member can develop their gift of teaching, and it also will make them study harder during the week. Or, each week the same person could share the summary.

3. After the summary has been given, the leader for that week will facilitate discussions through the rest of the reflection questions and select homework questions that apply to the group.

4. After discussion, the group will share prayer requests and pray for one another.

The strength of the study group is the fact that the members will be required to prepare their responses before the meeting, which will allow for easier discussion. In addition, each member will be given the opportunity to teach, which will further equip their ministry skills. The study group model has distinct advantages.

Reflection Questions

Writing is one of the best ways to learn. In class, we take notes and write papers, and these methods are used to help us learn and retain the material. The same is true with the Word of God. Obviously, all of the authors of Scripture were writers. This helped them better learn the Scriptures and also enabled them to more effectively teach it. In studying God's Word with the *Bible Teacher's Guide*, take time to write so you can similarly grow both in your learning and teaching.

1. How would you summarize the main points of the text/chapter? Write a brief summary.

2. What stood out to you most in the reading? Did any of the contents trigger any memories or experiences? If so, please share them.

3. What follow-up questions did you have about the reading? What parts did you not fully agree with?

4. What applications did you take from the reading, and how do you plan to implement them into your life?

5. Write several commitment statements in this format: *As a result of my time studying God's Word, I will* . . .

6. What are some practical ways to pray as a result of studying the text? Spend some time ministering to the Lord through prayer.

Walking the Romans Road

How can a person be saved? From what is he saved from? How can someone have eternal life? Scripture teaches that after death each person will spend eternity either in heaven or hell. How can a person go to heaven?

Paul said this to Timothy:

> But as for you, continue in what you have learned and have become convinced of, because you know those from whom you learned it, and how from infancy you have known the holy Scriptures, which are *able to make you wise for salvation through faith in Christ Jesus.*
> 2 Timothy 3:14-15

One of the reasons God gave us Scripture is to make us wise for salvation. This means that without it nobody can know how to be saved. This is why God gave us the Scripture.

Well then, how can a people be saved and what are they being saved from? A common method of sharing the good news of salvation is through the Romans Road. One of the great themes, not only of the Bible, but specifically of the book of Romans is salvation. In Romans, the author, Paul clearly details the steps we must take in order to be saved.

How can we be saved? What steps must we take?

Step One: We Must Accept that We Are Sinners

Romans 3:23 says, "for all have sinned and fall short of the glory of God." What does it mean to sin? The word sin means "to miss the mark." The mark we missed is looking like God. When God created mankind in the Genesis narrative, he created man in the "image of God" (1:27). The "image of God" means many things, but probably, most importantly it means we were made to be holy just as he is holy. Man was made moral. We were meant to reflect God's holiness in every way: the way we think, the way we talk, and the way we act. And any time we miss the mark in these areas, we commit sin.

Furthermore, we not only sin when we commit a sinful act such as: lying, stealing, or cheating. Again, we sin anytime we have a wrong heart motive. The greatest commandments in Scripture are to, "Love God with all our heart, mind, and soul and to love others as ourselves" (Matt 22:36-40, paraphrase). Whenever we don't love God supremely and love others as ourselves, we sin and fall short of the glory of God. For this reason, man is always in a state of sinning. Sadly, even if our actions are good, our heart is bad. I have never loved God with my whole heart, mind, and soul and neither has anybody else. Therefore, we have all sinned and fall short of the glory of God (Rom 3:23). We have all missed the mark of God's holiness and we must accept this.

What's the next step?

Step Two: We Must Understand We Are Under the Judgment of God

Why are we under the judgment of God? It is because of our sins. Scripture teaches God is not only a loving God, but he is just God. And his justice requires judgment for each of our sins. Romans 6:23 says: "For the wages of sin is death."

A wage is something we earn. Every time we sin, we earn the wage of death. What is death? Death really means separation. In physical death, the body is separated from the spirit, but in spiritual death, man is separated from God. Man currently lives in a state of spiritual death (cf. Eph 2:1-3). We do not love God, obey him, or know him as we should. Therefore, man is in a state of death.

Moreover, one day at our physical death, if we have not been saved, we will spend eternity separated from God in a very real hell. In hell, we will pay the wage for each of our sins. Therefore, in hell people will experience various degrees of punishment (cf. Lk 12:47-48). This places man in a very dangerous predicament—unholy and therefore under the judgment of God.

How should we respond to this? This leads us to our third step.

Step Three: We Must Recognize God Has Invited All to Accept His Free Gift of Salvation

Romans 6:23 does not stop at the wages of sin being death. It says, "For the wages of sin is death, but the gift of God is eternal life through Jesus Christ our Lord." Because God loved everybody on the earth, he offered the free gift of eternal life, which anyone can receive through Jesus Christ.

Because it is a gift, it cannot be earned. We cannot work for it. Ephesians 2:8-9 says, "For it is by grace you have been saved, through faith—and this not from yourselves, it is the gift of God—not by works, so that no one can boast."

Going to church, baptism, giving to the poor, or any other righteous work does not save. Salvation is a gift that must be received from God. It is a gift that has been prepared by his effort alone.

How do we receive this free gift?

Step Four: We Must Believe Jesus Christ Died for Our Sins and Rose from the Dead

If we are going to receive this free gift, we must believe in God's Son, Jesus Christ. Because God loved us, cared for us, and didn't want us to be separated from him eternally, he sent his Son to die for our sins. Romans 5:8 says, "But God demonstrates his own love for us in this: While we were still sinners, Christ died for us." Similarly, John 3:16 says: "For God so loved the world that he gave his only begotten son that whosoever believeth in him should not perish but have eternal life." God so loved us that he gave his only Son for our sins.

Jesus Christ was a real, historical person who lived 2,000 years ago. He was born of a virgin. He lived a perfect life. He was put to death by the Romans and the Jews. And he rose again on the third day. In his death, he took our sins and God's wrath for them and gave us his perfect righteousness, so we could be accepted by God. Second Corinthians 5:21 says: "God made him who had no sin to be sin for us, so that in him we might become the righteousness of God." God did all this so we could be saved from his wrath.

Christ's death satisfied the just anger of God over our sins. When God saw Jesus on the cross, he saw us and our sins and therefore judged Jesus. And now, when God sees those who are saved, he sees his righteous Son and accepts us. In salvation, we have become the righteousness of God.

If we are going to be saved, if we are going receive this free gift of salvation, we must believe in Christ's death, burial, and resurrection for our sins (cf. 1 Cor 15:3-5, Rom 10:9-10). Do you believe?

Step Five: We Must Confess Christ as Lord of Our Lives

Romans 10:9-10 says,

> That if you confess with your mouth, "Jesus is Lord," and believe in your heart that God raised him from the dead, you will be saved. For it is with your heart that you believe and are justified, and it is with your mouth that you confess and are saved.

Not only must we believe, but we must confess Christ as Lord of our lives. It is one thing to believe in Christ but another thing to follow Christ. Simple belief does not save. Christ must be our Lord. James said this, "Even the demons believe and shudder" (James 2:19) but the demons are not saved—Christ is not their Lord.

Another aspect of making Christ Lord is *repentance*. Repentance really means a change of mind that leads to a change of direction. Before we met Christ, we were living our own life and following our own sinful desires. But when we get saved, there is a change of mind and direction. We start to follow Christ as Lord.

How do we make this commitment to the lordship of Christ so we can be saved? Paul said we must confess with our mouth "Jesus is Lord" as we believe in him. Romans 10:13 says, "Everyone who calls on the name of the Lord will be saved."

If you admit that you are a sinner and understand you are under God's wrath because of them; if you believe Jesus Christ is the Son of God, that he died on the cross for your sins, and rose from the dead for your salvation; if you are ready to turn from your sin and cling to Christ as Lord, you can be saved.

If this is your heart, then you can pray this prayer and commit to following Christ as your Lord.

Dear heavenly Father, I confess I am a sinner and have fallen short of your glory, what you made me for. I believe Jesus Christ died on the cross to pay the penalty for my sins and rose from dead so I can have eternal life. I am turning away from my sin and accepting you as my Lord and Savior. Come into my life and change me. Thank you for your gift of salvation.

Scripture teaches that if you truly accepted Christ as your Lord, then you are a new creation. Second Corinthians 5:17 says, "Therefore, if anyone is in Christ, he is a new creation; the old has gone, the new has come!" God has forgiven your sins (1 John 1:9), he has given you his Holy Spirit (Rom 8:15), and he is going to disciple you and make you into the image of his Son (cf. Rom 8:29). He will never leave you nor forsake you (Heb 13:5), and he will complete the work he has begun in your life (Phil 1:6). In heaven, angels and saints are rejoicing because of your commitment to Christ (Lk 15:7).

Praise God for his great salvation! May God keep you in his hand, empower you through the Holy Spirit, train you through mature believers, and use you to build his kingdom! "The one who calls you is faithful, he will do it" (1 Thess 5:24). God bless you!

Coming Soon to the *BTG* Series

Available:
First Peter
Theology Proper
Building Foundations for a Godly Marriage
Colossians
Nehemiah
Philippians
Armor of God
The Perfections of God

Coming Soon:
Abraham
Ephesians

About the Author

Greg Brown earned his MA in religion and MA in teaching from Trinity International University, a MRE from Liberty University, and a PhD in theology from Louisiana Baptist University. He has served over eleven years in pastoral ministry and currently serves as chaplain and visiting professor at Handong Global University, pastor at Handong International Congregation, and as a Navy Reserve chaplain.

Greg married his lovely wife Tara Jayne in 2006, and they have one daughter, Saiyah Grace. He enjoys going on dates with his wife, playing with his daughter, reading, writing, studying in coffee shops, working out, and following the NBA and UFC. His pursuit in life, simply stated, is "to know God and to be found faithful by Him."

To connect with Greg, please follow at http://www.pgregbrown.com.

Notes

[1] The following point headings were adapted from Bruce Goettsche's sermon on Colossians 3:18-19, *Marriage God's Way*, accessed 3/22/15. http://www.unionchurch.com/archive/090698.html .

[2] "Discipline", accessed 2/7/15. http://dictionary.reference.com/browse/discipline .

[3] W. Barclay, *The New Daily Study Bible: The Letters to Philippians, Colossians, and Thessalonians*, 3rd ed. (Louisville, KY; London: Westminster John Knox Press, 2003), 190.

[4] Keathley, J. III., *The Principle of Nature (Knowing Your Child)*, accessed 2/8/15. https://bible.org/seriespage/principle-nature-knowing-your-child .

[5] Keathley, J. III. The Principle of Nature (Knowing Your Child), accessed 2/8/15 https://bible.org/seriespage/principle-nature-knowing-your-child .